# THE Crowdfunding
## B I B L E

# W H A T   T H E Y ' R E   S A Y I N G

"Every entrepreneur thinking about jumping into the wild world of crowdfunding needs to read this."

– J. Jennings Moss, Editor, Portfolio.com

"A must-read for anyone who wants to use the power of people, the Internet and social media to get projects off the ground."

– Rich DeMuro, Tech Reporter, KTLA-TV

"Don't start a crowdfunding campaign without it! "

– Brian Fargo, Creator, *Wasteland 2*

"A comprehensive look at the benefits and, more importantly, the potential pitfalls of crowdfunding that any developer ought to read before getting started."

- James Brightman, US Editor, GamesIndustry International

STRATEGIC CONSULTING | PRODUCT TESTING | MARKET RESEARCH | EXPERT WITNESSES

**www.TechSavvyGlobal.com**

As Seen On:

# ADDITIONAL RESOURCES:

**FREE BOOK FOR DOWNLOAD:**
## SMALL BUSINESS TIPS, TECH TRENDS, AND ONLINE MARKETING ADVICE
**www.ASmallBusinessExpert.com**

SOCIAL MEDIA CONSULTANTS:
FACEBOOK, TWITTER, GOOGLE+ (PLUS), YOUTUBE AND MORE
**www.ASocialMediaExpert.com**

WORK, LIFE AND FAMILY TIPS
PRODUCT NEWS, REVIEWS AND TRENDS
**www.TechSavvyMag.com**

Published By:

read.me

A NEW CHAPTER IN HIGH-TECH PUBLISHING

# WRITERS WANTED
## FOR TECHNOLOGY AND BUSINESS BOOKS

www.BooksAboutTechnology.com

# THE CROWDFUNDING BIBLE:
## HOW TO RAISE MONEY FOR ANY STARTUP, VIDEO GAME, OR PROJECT

## SCOTT STEINBERG

With
**Rusel DeMaria**

Edited by
**Jon Kimmich**

# THE CROWDFUNDING BIBLE:

## HOW TO RAISE MONEY FOR ANY STARTUP, VIDEO GAME, OR PROJECT

All Rights Reserved © 2012 by Overload Entertainment, LLC

No part of this book may be reproduced or transmitted in any form or by any means – graphic, electronic or mechanical – including photocopying, recording, taping or by any information storage retrieval system, without the written permission of the publisher.

LIMIT OF LIABILITY/DISCLAIMER OF WARRANTY: THE PUBLISHER AND THE AUTHOR MAKE NO WARRANTIES OR REPRESENATIONS REGARDING THE ACCURACY OR COMPLETENESS OF THE CONTENTS OF THIS WORK AND SPECIFICALLY DISCLAIM ALL WARRANTIES, INCLUDING WITHOUT LIMITATION WARRANTIES OF FITNESS FOR A PARTICULAR PURPOSE. THE ADVICE AND STRATEGIES CONTAINED HEREIN MAY NOT BE SUITABLE FOR EVERY SITUATION. THIS WORK IS SOLD WITH THE UNDERSTANDING THAT THE PUBLISHER AND AUTHOR ARE NOT ENGAGED IN RENDERING PROFESSIONAL SERVICES SUCH AS LEGAL, ACCOUNTING OR OTHER. IF PROFESSIONAL ASSISTANCE IS REQUIRED, A COMPETENT PROFESSIONAL PERSON SHOULD BE CONSULTED. NEITHER THE PUBLISHER NOR THE AUTHOR SHALL BE LIABLE FOR DAMAGES ARISING HEREFROM. THE FACT THAT AN ORGANIZATION OR WEBSITE IS REFERRED TO IN THIS WORK AS A CITATION AND/OR A POTENTIAL SOURCE OF FURTHER INFORMATION DOES NOT MEAN THAT THE AUTHOR OR THE PUBLISHER ENDORSES THE INFORMATION THAT THE ORGANIZATION OR WEBSITE MAY PROVIDE OR RECOMMENDATIONS IT MAY MAKE. FURTHER, INTERNET WEBSITES LISTED IN THIS WORK MAY HAVE CHANGED OR DISAPPEARED BETWEEN THE TIME THIS WORK WAS WRITTEN AND WHEN IT IS READ. NO WARRANTY MAY BE CREATED OR EXTENDED BY SALES OR PROMOTIONAL MATERIALS.

ISBN #: 978-1-105-72628-6

To order copies or to request permission to reprint, contact the publisher at:

Published by READ.ME
info@asmallbusinessexpert.com
www.asmallbusinessexpert.com

# DEDICATION

To Z, for whom endless possibilities await, and every aspiring entrepreneur
– with barriers to market entry rapidly crumbling, there's no better time to
act than the present. As dozens of enterprising new creators and startups are
proving, General Electric's not the only with the power to bring good things to
life: Get out there and start something today.

# FOREWORD

There's no denying that crowdfunding represents a fundamental change in the way that technologies, products and entrepreneurs are evaluated. Until recently, a relatively small number of very wealthy individuals held the purse strings of the creative world. Venture capitalists and angels were the gatekeepers to Silicon Valley, and they were quite selective. Innovation and creativity yearned for realization, and countless opportunities and ideas were lost forever – but out of the need for innovation came innovation itself. Just as the PC brought computers to the masses, so too does crowdfunding put funding for innovation in the hands of, well… the crowd.

Crowdfunding remains a financial instrument in transition. It's impossible to say what it will look like in five years, but it is equally difficult to envision a future without crowdfunding. After pounding the pavement and meeting various investors, I thought that I would not be able to carry through with my plan for Pebble. Just a few years ago it would have been dead without the support of investors. But thanks to Kickstarter and crowdfunding, and the tens of thousands of people who helped back us, my innovation is coming to life, and I hope the world will be a better place as a result.

My journey is exactly why crowdfunding is so important: Innovation cannot be lost to a VC's inbox. Innovation is too important for one man, or one firm, to pass judgment on. My innovation is not a world-changer, and yet fifty thousand people gave me millions of yeses when I couldn't even get a venture capital firm to give me a single no. Innovation serves and benefits the masses, and deserves to be judged by them. Crowdfunding may not yet be totally there yet, but I for one am excited to see what its future holds.

– Eric Migicovsky

# An Introduction to Crowdfunding

**W**ant to start your own business or have a great idea for tomorrow's next million-dollar invention? Congratulations – crowdfunding gives you the power to bring entire businesses and better widgets to life overnight. But what is crowdfunding exactly, how does it compare to crowdsourcing, and (more importantly) how can you use it to provide venture capital for any project or startup? In this book you'll find some handy hints, tips and how-to guides, as well as commentary from leading experts and crowdfunding veterans, to harnessing the ultimate in people power.

Following is a detailed overview of guiding business principles and case studies that you, as a modern entrepreneur, can utilize to create your own successful crowdfunding campaign. Note that while many examples here may come from the video games and interactive entertainment industry (among the fields that have benefited most financially from this practice), they're also applicable to many other consumer-facing sectors, including consumer electronics, periodicals, books, film, television, fashion and even special events and community projects. Worth keeping in mind too: As we go to press, close to $10 million in project funding has been raised in the last three months within the games industry alone, with success stories including Double Fine ($3.3M), Wasteland 2 ($2.9M+), Shadowrun Returns ($1.4M+) and more. Given the volume of public attention and dollars such campaigns have attracted, it's fully anticipated that this growth curve will continue in virtually every vertical – at least for the foreseeable future.

The good news for aspiring inventors and startups: With the right project and assets to convey your vision to potential backers, and a detailed understanding of how to engage with today's audiences, anyone can make their dreams a reality. Better yet, you too can participate in this exciting new means of funding, and launch nearly any promising new project or business. Ready to dive in headfirst and begin raising attention and capital for your latest and greatest ideas? Let's begin by taking a deeper look at what crowdfunding means, and how exactly the field works.

## What is Crowdfunding?

Simply put, crowdfunding is the process of asking the general public for donations that provide startup capital for new ventures. Using the technique, entrepreneurs and small business owners can bypass venture capitalists and angel investors entirely and instead pitch ideas straight to everyday Internet users, who provide financial backing. (At the same time, you will also gain early validation of project concepts and the projected scope of target markets.) Using services like Kickstarter and IndieGogo, creators essentially build web pages that host information, photos and promotional videos on products, projects or services they're looking to get funded. Viewers are then offered special rewards in exchange for pledges that support their efforts. Rather than equity or a share of profits though, benefits often take the form of exclusive merchandise, advance access to new releases, or more personal incentives. In the case of a movie, for example, donating $20 might get you a copy of the DVD, $50 a signed poster, and $500 an executive producer credit. For a larger donation (say, $2500), you might get a personal handwritten thank you note from the director, invite to an exclusive launch party, or even a bit part in the movie itself.

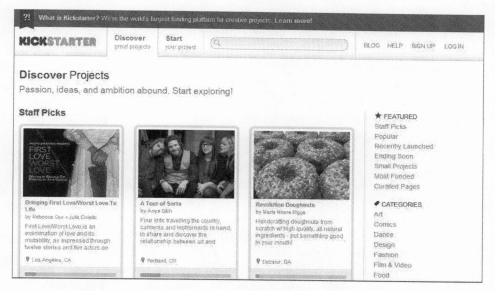

An offshoot of crowdsourcing – a business practice that involves asking user communities to submit ideas or contributions, e.g. possible designs for your firm's new logo – crowdfunding has recently grown in popularity. Many small projects have gotten the support they've needed to get off the ground, while a few very high-profile projects, such as Double Fine's new adventure game (which netted its first million in just 24 hours and turned the heads of many hopeful game developers) are quickly kicking down the doors for larger, full-scale ventures.

# Advantages of the Crowdfunding Model

Crowdfunding doesn't just help you finance your projects – it also lets you gauge public interest before launching new products or inadvertently spending millions on goods destined to collect dust in a warehouse. Some even say it's the best thing to happen to business since Apple's App Store. More important to note though is that you don't have to be a large, successful business to tap into its power – and that nearly any venture from art exhibitions to charity fundraisers can benefit. Whether looking to boost interest in a new neighborhood record store or skate park, or your grandkids' school fair, even everyday individuals can enjoy the heightened support and publicity such campaigns bring.

Furthermore, this strategy not only allows you to gauge the scope of general consumer interest in, and test the validity of, new concepts. It also gives you a direct conduit to shoppers, including those who are willing early financial supporters, and consequently the likeliest to spend more on updates and future releases. (A value proposition that becomes even more attractive if your product incorporates opportunities for the post-release purchase of additional content, e.g. via add-ons, expansions and microtransactions…) As an added benefit, crowdfunding additionally allows you to start forging early and strong relationships with committed customers, who will ultimately become your product's top advocates upon release.

From an entrepreneur's standpoint, it's hard to argue with the results. Under typical scenarios, business owners make educated guesses about products that people will be interested in, and how much they'll be willing to buy. Using crowdfunding, they can instead test ideas at little up-front cost and then spend accordingly. What's more, crowdfunding provides a better way to generate interest in projects and pre-orders up-front. Not only are customers more emotionally invested in the development process, they're also more emotionally invested in the end result. Advance purchases also provide working capital to fuel production, and rewards offered in exchange for fans' support provide a positive way to give back to deserving contributors. Best of all, crowdfunding lets you launch big ideas with next to no advance costs, and launch them right from your kitchen table. Even better, you can monitor and manage the process from your home computer, laptop or even your iPad.

Another significant advantage of crowdfunding is that you don't give away any ownership or equity stake in the venture. Traditional sources of investment typically require that you give up a portion of a company or project in exchange for their support. Moreover, investors frequently expect a quick return on investment (ROI), often at odds with entrepreneurs' focus on long-term value creation – and can even influence your project in ways you hadn't anticipated, and sometimes don't welcome. In contrast to the crowdfunding model, which affords backers no formal creative or commercial power over your project, traditional investment models, and investors, can often hold your feet to the fire at any time.

Here are some pros and cons to crowdfunding vs. traditional investment vehicles:

# Crowdfunding Pros

👤 You control everything, including costs, timing, delivery, creative vision and execution, marketing and customer interactions.

👤 You keep your equity: Projects and businesses remain 100% yours.

👤 You get to test and prove out the popularity of your model, using as little as a prototype or preproduction materials.

👤 You may also be able to test elements of your product's marketing approach and how well individual promotional aspects or overarching campaigns resonate with target consumers.

👤 You can sometimes make much more than you ever intended, or asked for. Under traditional investment scenarios, entrepreneurs must typically supply detailed business plans and budgets that justify their funding requests, negotiate the transfer of ownership stakes, and haggle over the actual value of their enterprise. Some companies and projects may require multiple rounds of funding, each of which demands additional negotiations and compromises, with the added risk (and stress) of having to prove the validity and worth of your project at each step. With crowdfunding, if your product resonates strongly with your audience, you may well exceed your funding target. Successful campaigns have raised as much as 4x or even 8x their original funding goals.

👤 Lucky or well-run crowdfunding projects can begin sourcing contributions with as little as a polished pitch – and may exceed funding goals many times over, without having to justify each additional dollar contributed. (*Caveat: Such scenarios are not necessarily the norm, but happen often enough to take into consideration when debating which investment channels to use.*) Unlike traditional investment ventures, which adhere closely to predefined game plans and budgets, some projects may even grow in feature set, scope and/or ambition with the extra money generated. One point to be aware of, however: As the market for pre-retailing your product develops, the bar will be raised as to what customers expect in terms of "sales materials" for crowdfunding efforts. You should always benchmark your project materials against those of similar campaigns in your chosen field or genre.

👤 If at first you don't succeed… Should you fail to meet your goal, you lose nothing (other than time and the occasional dent to your public image) and can try again, with an improved plan and presentation. Generally, if you fail to impress investors, you can consider yourself very lucky if they'll give you a second chance. Bear in mind when considering rebooting campaigns, though: If you are targeting the same customers or audience, they may well remember your earlier campaign, and its failure may have negative consequences.

👤 You can pre-sell your product or service, and depending on the costs associated with it, you may be able to get more than the actual retail value from backers who believe in your project. You're also mitigating risk and earning capital that can be directly applied towards production and marketing costs at the same time.

👤 An unexpected benefit of crowdfunding campaigns is that you will often receive very useful advice – and even tangible offers of assistance – from backers, who, after all, want you to succeed and will do everything they can to help you get there.

👤 Your backers become your built-in marketing team and crew of brand evangelists, helping to promote your project to all their friends and contacts.

# Crowdfunding Cons

👤 It's stressful. Talk to almost anyone who has run a crowdfunding project, and they'll tell you that running a campaign isn't easy, and that it's usually filled with unexpected ups and downs – even when successful. On the emotional roller coaster scale, think Space Mountain… not the kiddie rides.

👤 Plotting successful crowdfunding ventures demands a different kind of preparation than traditional product pitches. You're reaching out to end consumers, not professional investors – a completely different and far more diverse audience. This may require knowledge of consumer marketing, social networks and social marketing techniques in order to converse with these customers, as well as some familiarity with customer acquisition and conversion as well.

👤 It puts you and your ideas out directly in front of the public – and, potentially, the line of fire. Crowdfunding isn't for the faint of heart or the terminally bashful. There's also no opportunity to operate in stealth mode, meaning that competitors may be able to capitalize on public knowledge of your company or product.

👤 Success requires investing tireless effort into ongoing social marketing campaigns, and constant self-promotion, throughout the entire duration of the fundraising campaign. If you're shy, guarded or soft-spoken by nature, you'll have to get over these tendencies to run a successful crowdfunding campaign – or find someone else to serve as a project spokesperson.

👤 It requires that you be very creative about drumming up interest in your project, and it means you will be constantly looking for new ways to publicize, promote and otherwise call attention to your campaigns and surrounding efforts.

👤 It doesn't always work. That's not to say that you should be discouraged about the chances of successfully crowdfunding a project, but you do have to be realistic, and prepare yourself for potential failure. This often means having to have a Plan B – and C, D, etc.

👤 Crowdfunding requires that your project – whatever its theme, scope or contents – be something that interests a sufficient number of people strongly enough to motivate them to part with hard-earned cash. Part of the process of evaluating whether to undertake a crowdfunding effort is to take a careful, critical look at your project and assess the size of the potential audience to whom it will appeal, as well as the perceived value it will bring them. When you are executing the campaign, you'll have to target this market specifically, and you'll need to strategize how to engage them where they consume media, news, opinions and insights on a regular, running basis – no small task.

👤 With crowdfunding, you assume responsibility for dealing with an often larger and potentially more diverse set of backers than under traditional investment scenarios – all of whom may have differing expectations and demands. Likewise, few examples exist thus far that illustrate the ramifications of crowdfunded products that have not been released, or where a product was pitched and funded, but a wildly different product was ultimately released. Consider the potential impact to your projects, livelihood and business.

👤 Finally, no matter how interesting your project is, know that you will be competing against other projects – many of which may be vying for the same target audience, share of voice and pool of disposable income. And, as crowdfunding grows in popularity and notoriety, the commercial landscape will become even more competitive.

## THE REALITY OF CROWDFUNDING

**"If you think crowdfunding is easy, guess again: It's definitely not. It's actually pretty scary, because you have to be prepared to put yourself out there on display [for the public]. It's the Internet and you have to expect mixed feedback."**
Jane Jensen, *Pinkerton Road: A Year of Adventure*

## Kicking it Forward

Competition for crowdfunding dollars is already high, and destined to become even more competitive as time passes. Sometimes it pays to give back: That's why Brian Fargo, whose successful Wasteland 2 campaign earned nearly $3 million, recommends embracing the Kick It Forward concept – a pledge by those who've successfully crowdfunded ventures to donate 5% of the profits (after shipping and expenses) from their finished projects to fund other crowdfunding projects. In his own words:

"Any developer that puts the "Kicking it Forward" badge on their Kickstarter project page is agreeing that they will put 5% of their finished product profits back into other Kickstarter projects. To be abundantly clear, this is only money that the developer earns as profit AFTER the project ships and AFTER they have paid their expenses. This is NOT a suggestion to invest money they received from people who invested into their project via Kickstarter."

Note that while the concept of Kicking It Forward started on Kickstarter, it may quickly spread to other crowdfunding sites under a variety of different names and forms. This ingenious idea helps assure that more projects will get funded in the future, allowing the backers of projects that support Kicking It Forward to offer continued support to the crowdfunding movement. We recommend considering it for any campaign. Besides being a kind gesture that lets you also set a good example, positively give back to the community and help others meet their funding goals, the goodwill it generates can be priceless. Creators can use all the support they can get – and you yourself may even need to call in a favor yourself from them someday, drawing upon their connections, customers and/or business savvy.

## Traditional Investment Pros

👤 A relationship that's supposed to be strictly business: Each party clearly spells out and understands what's being offered in exchange for the other's support – duties and obligations, at least in theory, begin and end at what's on the signed contract.

👤 The scope of projects, as well as their general feature set and budgetary demands, are typically outlined at the outset of the relationship, and – for better or worse – cannot often deviate, because of the fixed nature of schedules, plans and funding. This allows for greater focus.

👤 You can get right down to work. Once you have secured funding, you are ready to begin diving into the business of running your business on a day to day basis.

👤 You get validation. Traditional investors often have extensive experience with the kinds of projects they fund, and don't fund projects they don't see a need for or personally believe in. So if you've pitched an investor successfully, you have already convinced one of the world's toughest and most demanding audiences that your ideas have merit.

👤 You often get support and expert advice. Wise investors will many times step in and offer you counsel or request (and unfortunately sometimes demand) a course correction if they see your business or leadership team floundering or headed in what they believe to be the wrong direction. Often, this advice is well worth considering. Likewise, it's important to remember that connections can be equally important as cash itself: Frequently, investors will open doors, make introductions and provide entrees to new clients or arenas worth several times their weight in gold.

👤 When things go well, and your project is moving forward, investors will actively do what they can to speed ventures along and help you succeed – assistance that shouldn't be discounted, given the considerable financial and professional clout they can often bring to bear.

## Traditional Investment Cons

👤 Under most scenarios, receiving investment from outside sources requires giving away equity in your intellectual property (IP) or project – and sometimes in your whole company – in order to secure financial backing. Other scenarios may see you having to forego a share of profits, pay a licensing fee on every transaction, or be forced to meet stringent project milestones or deliverables at the risk of losing funding, the IP being created or even the entire business itself.

👤 If you didn't raise enough to fund your project fully from initial investors, miscalculated budgetary needs or scheduling slips and development difficulties raise production costs, you may find yourself in an untenable position – and may end up scrambling to make payroll and/ or forced to give away more equity to secure additional funds from further sources. Note that crowdfunding can be a means of closing funding gaps without having to take on additional debt or incur another round of equity financing, though – should they be necessary – backers may be every bit as skeptical (if not more so) of secondary funding rounds as traditional investors.

👤 Investors operate on a timeline. Many look for a quick turnaround on their investment. While the actual amount of time varies by project, deal and individual preference, as a general rule, it pays to realize: They're not offering the equivalent of a 30-year home mortgage. In general, financial backers expect to make a high return on investment on funds placed into your project/ company in a short amount of time. This may or may not conform directly to your comfort zone, and may give investors' undue leverage over the venture – because they hold the money, they often hold the majority of the cards.

👤 As pointed out in the Pros section prior, advice and introductions provided by investors can often be very valuable. But it can sometimes be just as devastating as well, because outside parties' vision and goals for any venture don't necessarily align with your own. Investors ultimately want projects to go in a direction that realizes the maximum amount of profit for them in the least amount of time. Some may not afford you the time, support or freedom of creative vision you need to develop your project or company to its full potential – at least, insofar as you define success.

---

## THE BENEFITS OF CROWDFUNDING

"Crowdfunding was the best way that Wasteland 2 could have happened. Any other funding method would have had strings and people who had ideas attached to it. I believe that there's a direct correlation between developers with independence and quality. To be sure, the people at companies like Blizzard, Valve and other top software makers are very talented, but they also get to determine when projects are done. They do what they think is right."

-Brian Fargo, *Wasteland 2*

# Who Should Consider Crowdfunding?

## IMPROVING YOUR CHANCES OF SUCCESS

"To improve chances of success, you want to build a project or product where you think you're filling a hole. Part of the trick is showing people things that they either a) haven't seen in a long time or b) things they haven't seen before."

-Brian Fargo, *Wasteland 2*

There are several factors to consider if you are thinking about using a crowdfunding model to finance a business, product, project, service or event.

1. How good is your idea – really? Are you certain that people will be interested in it?
2. Why is your product, service or venture destined to sell – what value does it offer the customer?
3. What differentiates your project from existing competitors, or alternatives that have come before? Are you utilizing an existing brand, IP or personality that has a pre-existing base of fans or consumers? (Using an existing, if perhaps older, brand or IP which consumers have fond memories of can be a very effective strategy.)
4. Can you express your idea simply and at the same time get people excited about it? If not, it may be that the idea isn't all that compelling, or that you may not be the right person to communicate or present it.
5. Do you have something tangible to show when presenting your venture – some visual aspect of your project that can help other people visualize it?
6. How well do you know and understand your target audience?
7. Do you have confidence in your ability to reach out and connect with potential backers? Have you planned which vehicles you will use to reach out and connect with them?
8. Have you calculated just how much money you need – truly need – to get your ideas off the ground?
9. Have you factored in all financial variables, including the costs of reward fulfillment, payments to the crowdfunding service, and taxes?
10. Have you been sensible enough to build a budget that allows for breathing room in certain areas, and factors in conservative projections?
11. Are you positive that you can fulfill all your promises, including completing the project in the allotted timeframe, and delivering on all features and content covered in your pitch? Have you considered the impact on your product's brand identity, or your own personal brand, should your campaign not succeed?
12. Do you have some great rewards in mind to give backers and fans incentive to donate?

Have you mapped out your reward tiers? How will you offer these rewards, and what dollar amount will you attach to them?

13. Can you offer meaningful rewards at a variety of investment levels to attract all potential patrons?
14. What specific or unique rewards will you use to get people talking? Can you create any singular ones that can be utilized in social media campaigns or for press outreach?
15. Do you understand all the personal and professional demands that the process of running a crowdfunding campaign demands from creators? Are you prepared to put 110% effort into making your crowdfunding project a success?
16. Do you have at least some marketing, public relations and social media connections and savvy?
17. What promotional campaign activities do you plan to pursue leading up to and during launch? How will you keep the buzz going after your crowdfunding project debuts?
18. Are you ready and able to take a big personal risk?
19. Do you – and at least a few other people you can look to for support, whether financial, emotional or otherwise – fully believe in your project?
20. Who can you turn to for help, whether in terms of assistance with asset creation, financial backing, raising awareness or just help spreading the word?

**Most importantly**: Have you examined other crowdfunding projects – both successes and failures – to understand which approaches, techniques and strategies work or tend to result in failure?

If you can satisfactorily answer all of these questions with a straight face, and believe with certainty in your ability to deliver on all, there's a good chance that you can be successful, if you follow the guidelines you'll find later in this book.

---

## DON'T BE FOOLED

"Crowdfunding isn't for all projects, or projects of all sizes. With the success of crowdfunding, should a publisher of Activision's size suddenly say, let's go do the next *Call of Duty* on Kickstarter, or offer a super-long pre-sale? Not likely. In the end, smaller teams [and projects] make more sense for the format."

-Jordan Weisman, *Shadowrun Returns*

---

# Preparing for Your Crowdfunding Adventure

**B**efore you jump into the deep waters of crowdfunding, it's important to learn how to swim. Take a tip from the Boy Scouts and always be prepared: Or, to continue with the metaphors, first discover how to crawl before you run – and, as experienced crowd-funders might warn, also be ready, willing and able to pick yourself back up when you accidentally sprint headfirst into a waiting pitfall.

## Two Ways to Crowdfund

Before you can even begin your crowdfunding venture, you have some important decisions to make. Chief among them is deciding exactly how you will fund your project through public support. When it comes to raising capital through outreach to public donors, you essentially have two choices:

**Option 1:** Use an existing crowdfunding service, such as:

Kickstarter
IndieGogo
Spacehive
RocketHub
Ulule
33Needs
Spot.us
Community Funded
Crowdcube
Peerbackers
Grow VC
8-Bit Funding

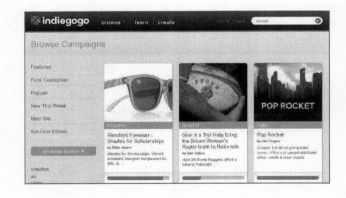

**Option 2:** Utilize your own website, software platform and existing network of connections to provide unique campaigns built around special offers, incentives and community efforts that convince backers to help fund your project.

Option 2 requires that you possess a user-friendly, accessible and stable solution for promoting and processing pledge efforts, as well as the capability to engage, motivate and retain the attention of a sizable fan base that believes in your brand, your company or your project. For instance, small New Zealand company Grinding Gears ran a closed beta of its action role-playing game (RPG) project Path of Exile for several months, after which it sent out a message to all the title's beta testers with special offers in exchange for donations, such as access to open beta programs for friends of backers or additional in-game cash at launch. In addition to the project's supporting Kickstarter campaign, classic adventure game maker and author Jane Jensen is also trying a unique approach with her new studio Pinkerton Road's "community supported" gaming model. (Based on community supported agriculture, instead of a basket of freshly-picked produce each month, those who pledge $50 or more receive all games the developer produces for one year.) Going forward, these and other creative funding solutions, such as Slightly Mad's *World of Mass Development* funding platform (developers submit ideas and projects to the community for backing, advice and feedback) or Gambitious (a European service that lets investors buy shares in game projects that pay potential dividends), will undoubtedly proliferate. However, unless your project or team has a large existing built-in audience of fans, or the ability to self-motivate large crowds, for most people, using one of the crowdfunding services found detailed under Option 1 will likely prove more productive.

---

## BUILDING YOUR OWN CROWDFUNDING PLATFORM

**"Why did we choose to create our own crowdfunding platform instead of using another service?**

   **a) Our project has already had millions of dollars spent on it, rather than being an idea that we could do if we had the money.**
   **b) We want to be able to give people the access to the game that they're buying immediately, rather than making them wait a month.**
   **c) We already have an established fan base, so we don't have to rely on [outside] traffic.**

**In our case we already had a product and fan base. They were just using it to pre-order microtransaction credit that they'd be buying eventually."**

-Chris Wilson, *Path of Exile*

---

## TAKING A HYBRID APPROACH

**"We had the idea for a consumer-supported gaming model where we wanted fans and players directly involved with the studio – a direct line of communication, if you will. Kickstarter looked to be a great vehicle for that and the mechanism for our first CSG (Community Supported Game) campaign."**

Jane Jensen, *Pinkerton Road: A Year of Adventure*

---

# Research

Whatever your approach to crowdfunding, your first order of business is to take a hard, analytical look at projects that have succeeded, as well as ventures that have failed. Your goal: To observe and learn how successful projects work, and to understand the subtle nuances and tactics that determine why some triumph while others don't.

What to look for:

### The Product, Service or Event
- Is it something that the casual observer would find interesting?
- Is the venture compelling enough that people would pay to support it?
- What makes the product, service or offering unique or different?
- What value does the venture offer end consumers?
- What audience do you think this project was intended for?
- How big a target market do you think exists for it?
- What three key characteristics define the project?
- If you had to summarize the project in 20 seconds, how would you do so?

### The Pitch
- How did those making the pitch introduce their project?
- Did the creators clearly explain what the venture does, or the purpose it serves? In the case of creative ventures, apps or interactive products, were hands-on functionality, gameplay and/or key story elements well-explained? Did they paint an accurate picture in your mind of the project or product?
- Who does the pitch speak to?
- If you feel that you are amongst the target audience this campaign is supposed to appeal to, would YOU pay? Why or why not? Does this product solve a problem you have or provide a service you'd use?
- What made it compelling or not?
- What approach did the creators take to convey their message (humorous, serious, quirky, imaginative, straightforward, etc.)?
- How long did it take you to fully understand the project being described?
- Did you have to have any prior knowledge of the type of product, service or event to comprehend the material presented?
- How easy was it to skim and read the pitch?
- How many key details and features were described?
- How quickly did it take for the creators to cut to the chase and speak directly about project specifics and funding needs?
- At what point was a call to action (donate now!) included?

- How much personal vs. project information was presented?
- Were "goodwill" programs offered, i.e. the "Kicking it Forward" program on Kickstarter?
- How many updates were made during the course of the campaign?
- What was the nature of these updates? Were they simple notes and thank you messages; did they add new rewards and goals; or did they answer common questions presented by fans?

## The Video
- Was it interesting or boring?
- Natural or stiff/forced?
- Well-produced or amateurish (in a bad way)?
- Funny? Paced well? Engaging? Drawn out? Repetitive?
- Did you watch the entire performance?
- Were all your questions answered?
- How quickly were key selling points presented?
- How many (and which specific) project details were discussed?
- Did creators use words or pictures to tell the tale?
- How much of the project did you really see?
- How much actual footage of the project itself vs. individuals was included?
- What did you empathize most with: The individual or the venture itself?
- How long was the video?
- Did the clip end with a direct request?
- Did the video contain contact information?
- What, if anything, made you want to watch more?

## The Rewards
- Do the rewards make sense, and are they logical, based on the type of project?
- Are there enough rewards at different payment tiers?
- Do rewards offer enough value for the money? Why so/not?
- Is there a smooth transition from low value rewards to very high-value/high-donation rewards?
- Was more actual merchandise offered or personal/professional rewards? How much physical merchandise was used vs. virtual rewards?
- How many rewards allowed users to actually be a part of, or appear within, the actual project?
- How many rewards were limited in number? What was their distribution across funding tiers?
- What kinds of personal payouts – thank you calls from the lead singer, contributors' names included in the album liner notes, dinner with the band, etc. – were offered?
- You can see in a project that has been running a while, or that has completed, exactly

how many people picked specific rewards. Which rewards were most successful? Why? Which payment tiers and rewards were most popular based on number of backers?

- Were any unique rewards – i.e. dinner with a famous artist or software developer – offered? How popular were they in drumming up financial support or media attention?
- Were rewards fixed at the time of announcement, or more introduced later? At what point during the project's duration did they debut?
- Did fans contribute new rewards themselves?
- Did fans contribute new "stretch goals," and if so, were new rewards created to support these goals?
- Were any rewards exclusive or specific to the promotion itself?

## The Funding Goal
- Was it a reasonable goal from the beginning?
- For those projects that failed, why did they fail?
- Was their funding goal too high?
- Did they not get attention from press/fans or social media channels?
- Was the product not well presented or explained?
- Did the project's creators fail to engage fans while the project was running through regular updates and social media outreach?
- Were rewards not compelling?
- Some other factor?
- What funding ranges seem to be most successful? Why?
- For those projects that succeed wildly, what are the main factors that you think contributed to their success? Do any of them apply to you and your project? For instance:
    - The past success or notoriety of the people behind the project.
    - The existing fan base for the project.
    - The uniqueness and audience appeal of the project.
    - The exclusivity or uniqueness of rewards being offered.
    - The size of target audience vs. funding goal set.
    - The presentation of the project – both written and visual.
    - Other factors – what are they?
- What multiple of the original funding goal did the project finally reach?
- For successful products, did they offer stretch goals? What types of stretch goals were most successful? How was the community involved and how did fans respond?

## The Marketing and PR Campaign
- What advertising, marketing and public relations activities were utilized to promote the project?
- Where did creators focus their efforts – online/print/social media, or some combination thereof?

- Which tactics were most effective? Least?
- What kind of media attention did they attract, from whom, and what types of publications responded best and/or most frequently?
- How did fans and journalists react to various promotions?
- Which seemed to resonate best with the press and public? Why?
- Which activities generated the least response? Why?
- How often were new promotional campaigns introduced? When? What did they consist of?
- What kinds of assets were promoted? How many were provided with each new step in the campaign?
- How did creators engage with and motivate the fan community? How often did they make outreach, and through which channels?
- What tone of voice and types of materials did creators use when engaging with others? Did these differ between audiences? How so? How would you have done it differently?
- What type of fans seemed to most rally behind the project? Why so?
- What level of time, resources, money and manpower did creators invest in their campaigns?
- How did the project leverage the presence of key individuals (if the team behind it contains well-known "brand-name" members) throughout its duration?
- Did the team, before the campaign even launched, conduct press interviews and float the idea of a crowdfunding campaign to gauge fan response?

## Notable Game Projects

Although crowdfunding has been around a while, and there are several sites that support the model, a few high-profile video game projects in particular have recently helped catapult the concept into the public eye. Following are several of note which are well worth researching, as they may help to inspire new ideas and serve as useful reference points when plotting out pitches, rewards and funding levels.

## High-Profile Game Projects

**Double Fine Adventure**. Noted designer Tim Schafer's adventure game project on Kickstarter turned heads and may have single-handedly launched the virtual gold rush of crowdfunding projects when it received over $1 million in its first 24 hours. With a starting goal of a mere $400,000, Double Fine Adventure ultimately received more than $3.3 million in pledges. To date, this is the largest amount pledged for a crowdfunded game, though it's dwarfed by the over $8.5 million that's been pledged for the Pebble E-Paper Watch as of press time – the largest amount for any product of any kind on Kickstarter or any other crowdfunding site.

**Wasteland 2:** Interplay founder Brian Fargo's development studio InXile made $700,000 in its first 24 hours of pitching a sequel to highly-popular, but long out of print RPG *Wasteland*, ultimately raising nearly $3 million for the project.

**Shadowrun Returns**. From Harebrained Schemes and original designer Jordan Weisman, this modern sequel to the popular classic sci-fi meets fantasy role-playing title *Shadowrun* exceeded its $400,000 goal easily and at the time of this writing had generated $1.4 million in pledges with 5 days still to go.

**Leisure Suit Larry in the Land of the Lounge Lizards: 25th Anniversary Edition**. Infamous adventure game designer Al Lowe reappears as a driving force behind this sequel to the hilarious, long-running (but recently overlooked) libidinous adventure game series. Over 14,081 backers came together to donate $655,182 and make the dream a reality, despite creator Replay Games asking for only $500,000.

**The Banner Saga**. Pitched by Stoic Studios (which includes former *Star Wars: The Old Republic* team members), this is the company's first game as a new independent outfit. It has collected over $500,000 (5x its initial funding goal) thanks largely in part due to a compelling video piece that illustrates the art direction for the game.

## Smaller Game Projects

**Cognition: An Erica Reed Thriller**. A smaller project from budding adventure game developer Phoenix Online Studios, which asked for just $25K and ended up raising $34,000.

**Random Dungeon Generator as a Dungeon Map**. A role-playing game aid that was funded to the tune of nearly $28K – 1389% of its goal.

**TAKEDOWN**. A squad-based shooter from veteran developers behind titles like *Halo Reach* and *Ghost Recon*, this original game raised nearly $222K – 110% of its goal.

**FTL: Faster Than Light**. A "spaceship simulation Roguelike-like" that exceeded its goal by 2005% and earned $200K in pledges.

**Republique**. An iOS-exclusive game from team members behind *Halo* and *Metal Gear Solid* that's collected over $82,000 with 18 days remaining in its campaign as we go to press.

## Notable Consumer Products and Projects

While PC and video games have thus far proven most popular as crowdfunded projects, so too are other creative ventures such as books, movies, consumer electronics and public events increasing in popularity with backers. From unique and eye-catching gadgets to gripping adventure novels and documentary films that commemorate unique sub-cultures or periods in history, the list of successful ventures continues to grow. There are far too many to cover here, but below are a number of recent projects which caught the public eye – we suggest referencing all as a starting point when deciding how to best plot and execute your own venture.

**Pebble E-Paper Watch**. Billed as "the first watch built for the 21st century," this customizable timepiece interfaces with downloadable apps, the Internet and iPhone or Android smartphones to create a surprisingly fashionable, yet also highly personalized and connected experience. The most successful crowdfunding project seen to date, it's raised over $8.5 million dollars as we go to press, and continues to draw widespread attention from the media and general public.

**100 Yen: The Japanese Arcade Experience**. A full-length (75-minute) documentary film that chronicles the rise and evolution of both arcades and arcade culture in Japan, *100 Yen* far exceeded expectations on IndieGogo, raising $14,848 – much more than its $9000 goal. An extensive trailer and interviews with notables from the world of fandom were effectively utilized to mobilize backers to fund production of the movie.

**Glif – iPhone 4 Tripod**. A tripod mount for the iPhone that can also act as a kickstand for the handset – thereby enabling hands-free videoconferencing, filmmaking abilities, alarm clock features and other functions – this project proved an early success for crowdfunding in the consumer electronics space. Hoping to raise just $10,000, its creators instead brought in a whopping $137,417, and attracted considerable attention from enthusiast and mainstream media.

**Indie Game: The Movie**. Among the earliest film-based efforts on Kickstarter, this campaign – featuring a documentary about the independent video games movement – kicked off in May of 2010 and raised over $23,000 in pledges. A second campaign followed roughly a year later that increased the project's total take to nearly $100,000. Thanks in part to the attention it helped bring, the film was then optioned by HBO for development as a TV series, making it among the first crowdfunded movies to cross over into the mainstream video distribution world.

**TikTok+ LunaTik Multi-Touch Watch Kits**. Launched roughly a month after the Glif, this campaign – which promoted novel solutions for turning the iPod Nano into a personal wristwatch – was a pioneering record-setter on Kickstarter. Despite asking for only $15,000, its creators eventually raised over $1 million dollars through contributions on the service, and the product's own dedicated website.

**Designing Obama**. This 360-page book featuring art and design work from the Obama presidential campaign proved an initial example of how successful crowdfunding could prove when tapped to fund artistic works and cultural endeavors. Launched in 2009, it was assembled by Scott Thomas, the Design Director for the campaign which helped propel Obama into office.

**The Order of the Stick**. Many comic book creators turn to crowdfunding for support. But webcomic *The Order of the Stick*'s creator Rich Burlew can boast about being one of the scant few to have raised in excess of a million dollars. Built around bringing a popular out-of-print series back to shelves, it yielded over $1.25M in backing – and earned those contributions from nearly 15,000 backers.

# Before You Start...

Crowdfunding sounds easy (just put up a page on Kickstarter and watch the bucks roll in!), and on the surface, it may very well be so – at least in principle. But successful crowdfunding generally doesn't happen by accident. If you look at triumphant projects across the Web, you'll find that many share several attributes in common, including one or more of the following building blocks:

- A solid idea and sellable vision for the product or service
- Careful pre-planning and preparation
- A strong presentation, ideally coupled with high production values
- A reward structure that appeals to the project's audience
- Ongoing outreach to backers
- Effective social media, marketing and PR strategies
- The presence of a popular pre-existing brand or personality that's attached to the project, or an existing audience for the property.

To launch a successful crowdfunding campaign, you'll need several of the above foundations in place, plus a very clear idea of the costs involved and how you are going to keep your project fresh, top of mind, and growing in public awareness during the time it is active.

Another critical decision involves which of the many crowdfunding sites and services you will use. Assuming that you are not going to try to raise crowdsourced funds on your own, you will probably be turning to one of the following solutions. Keep in mind that platforms are not all the same in terms of feature set, audience size, credibility with consumers, and ultimate reach. Some may focus on specific types of projects, such as local or humanitarian efforts, while others are better suited to high-tech ventures or non-profits. For example: Spot.us is about collaborative journalism, not products. So while you have several choices here when picking a funding source, it's advisable that you take time to check each out and decide which fits your needs best.

To get you started, here are a few insights into some of the major crowdfunding sites. You can be sure that many new sites will appear now that several high-profile campaigns have caught people's attention, but the following solutions are already up and running:

## Kickstarter

The biggest of the crowdfunding sites, Kickstarter raised approximately $100 million in funding in 2011, and is on-track to raise upwards of $250 million or more in 2012. Kickstarter is open to any kind of project, anywhere in the world – but although anyone can be a funder, to create a campaign, you must have a U.S. presence and, theoretically, tax ID. Approval is required to launch a campaign. Kickstarter provides many levels of support from the time you begin developing your campaign until after it is completed. The site offers smooth integration into social media and individual websites, great online help, an analytics dashboard that helps you track your project progress and see where your pledges are coming from, and a post-campaign survey tool.

**Fees:** 5% if you meet goal. None if you don't. Processing fees from 3-5% via Amazon.
**Goals:** Meet goal or get nothing. You can keep anything over your goal, though fees still apply.

## IndieGogo

Open to any kind of project, anywhere in the world, IndieGogo offers a lot of tools and support to track your project. It's also helpful in that it offers the opportunity to keep money raised from campaigns that do not reach their goal. Smooth integration into social media and individual websites and a robust set of analytics tools to track your progress round out its benefits.

**Fees:** IndieGogo features two funding plans:
- Flexible. 4% if you meet goal, 9% if you don't, but you keep your money in either case.
- Fixed. 4% if you meet goal, no fees if you don't and you get nothing in the latter case – donations are returned to contributors.

**Goals:** Flexible or fixed plan. In flexible, you get whatever you earn. Fixed, meet goal or nothing, but you can keep anything you earn past the goal.

## RocketHub

Open to any kind of project. Includes more social concepts beyond funding (fueling) projects, including options to vote for projects and also to earn badges on the site. Creators can apply for

RocketHub's "LaunchPad Opportunities" separately from their projects. LaunchPad Opportunities are awarded to certain project builders based on their creations' popularity and the evaluation of expert judges, and can be quite valuable. Examples include the services of a publicist to help promote your project, or the opportunity for five winning photographers to exhibit their work in a prestigious New York gallery.

**Fees:** There appear to be no fees for projects. LaunchPad Opportunities are free to people who have run a successful project, $5 for anyone else who wants to enter.

**Goals:** You keep any money raised.

## Ulule

European/international focus, default funding in Euros, but supports other currency options. Also focused on projects that are "for the betterment of society." People can additionally "like" projects and the number of likes is displayed with the project listing. Approval required to launch a project.

**Fees:** 5% on funded projects plus 3.4% commission to PayPal and $0.25 per transaction. No charges for projects that are not fully funded.

**Goals:** Meet goal or get nothing. You can earn an unlimited amount past the initial goal.

## 33Needs

This crowdfunding service differs in several ways from other crowdfunding sites. Its primary strength comes in the form of profit sharing: In exchange for donations, backers are promised a percentage of profits for a set amount of time. This is especially relevant to entrepreneurs starting new ventures who are willing to share profits with backers, who are betting on the project's success and end up with a strong stake in the outcome. The focus is on business startups as opposed to other sites, which tend to be more project-oriented.

**Fees:** 5% plus transaction fees.

**Goals:** All or nothing. Can earn more than goal.

## Spot.us

A "community powered reporting" project that lets people present a "story" for which they seek funding, bringing together citizens, journalists and news organizations. Focus is on "local" reporting. Stories begin as "tips," short descriptions of the issue. A journalist can then take the tip and write a pitch, including the funding needed. All stories are available under the Creative Commons license, although news organizations can donate 50% or more to the project to gain a temporary copyright. Topics include Government + Politics, Local Science & Business, Race & Demographics, Consumer Protection and many more. Under current plans, 90% of money earned goes to the journalist and 10% to another journalist who serves as the editor. The upshot is that it gives journalists work and helps citizens identify stories that need to be covered.

**Fees:** None
**Goals:** All or nothing

## Spacehive

Spacehive's founder describes it as "an online funding platform for neighborhood improvement projects" – and primarily for those based in England at that. Approval is required to launch a campaign.

**Fees:** Scale with size of project. Money is in English Pounds.

**Goals:** Meet goal or get nothing. You can't earn more than the goal you set.

## Crowdcube

Based in the United Kingdom, serves as a platform for small investments in UK businesses and startups. Each project runs for 90 days. Equity in the company is given in exchange for donations. Incentive rewards are also recommended. Must be 18 or older and be legally able to create a UK based limited company to utilize.

**Fees:** £250 (currently waived) plus 5% of realized goal. Also £1750 in legal fees. No charges if the project fails to meet its goal.

**Goals:** Minimum £10,000 goal. No maximum. All or nothing.

    👤 Note: Donations in exchange for equity are legal in the UK, but not, at the time of this writing, in the U.S. That may soon change as President Obama recently passed the Jumpstart Our Business Startups (a.k.a. JOBS) Act (sometimes referred to in part as the CROWDFUND Act), which will allow entrepreneurs on sites like Kickstarter to offer equity in exchange for investment. However, as of press time, laws and regulations governing these investments have yet to be put into effect.

*Normally, when a company seeks financing from the public it must register as a security with the Securities and Exchange Commission, providing detailed disclosures. The CROWDFUND Act would provide an alternative to this process, allowing companies to raise up to $1,000,000 annually through crowdfunding on registered Internet websites. – Senator Jeff Merkeley (D-OR)*

## 8-Bit Funding

Dedicated exclusively to crowdfunding game projects. The model is similar to that of other crowdfunding sites and supports any kind of game, including video games, but also card and board games as well.

**Fees:** 5% of successful project for 8-Bit Funding and 2.9% + $0.30 per transaction.

**Goals:** All or nothing. You can keep whatever you generate, and you can restart a project if it doesn't succeed.

## Peerbackers

Founded in 2011, Peerbackers facilitates project fundraising for "entrepreneurs, innovators and trailblazers" and their ideas (rather than serving as a platform specifically to promote creative projects). Peerbackers reviews submissions for legitimacy and the applicants' understanding of how to be successful in crowdfunding. Like other sites, rewards are provided to backers in return for their participation. However, these rewards may not include the actual products under development (if the venture even has a consumer product associated it).

**Fees:** 5% plus Paypal charge (2.9%).

**Goals:** Three possible outcomes – 1) Project is fully or over-funded, and you keep what you make; 2) Project fails but you can still fulfill rewards – you keep what you've made; 3) Project fails and you cannot fulfill rewards – you make nothing and backers are refunded.

### Microryza

A project crowdfunding site based in Seattle that targets commercial (though largely geeky) science- and tech-related projects. Bills itself as "a new way to fund innovative research," helping pair backers with researchers looking to fund scientific studies, insights into global warming and other unique ventures. Features a strong emphasis on academic works and projects that expand the scientific and professional world's collective knowledge base and general frame of reference.

**Fees:** 10% of raised capital only on successful projects (includes a 3% transaction fee)

**Goals:** All or nothing

### Grow VC

Based in Hong Kong, with offices in the UK, US and Finland, Grow VC is a more complex site that allows startups to receive equity investments up to $1M per year. In addition to monetary investment, the site includes an "Experts" system in which someone with special abilities or knowledge can offer their "work investment" to a startup on the site. There are a lot more tools on this site for assessing the value and reputation of a startup. Also present is a "micro investment" model where investors can dedicate a monthly budget as low as $20 and Grow VC helps them by providing tools and profiles of startups, including their history.

**Fees:** 2.5% of raised capital only on successful projects

**Goals:** No information about how goals are handled.

# Benefits and Risks

The benefits of crowdsourcing should be obvious:

- You get money to help complete your project.
- You keep control of your equity as well as your creative independence.
- You get to gauge people's enthusiasm and interest in your project.
- You create empathy with fans and greater emotional investment in your product, brand and associated ventures.
- You can kick-start your marketing campaign and turn fans into brand evangelists.

- Backers feel as though they hold a personal stake in your project, making them automatically part of your social media and marketing teams.
- It's a handy way to raise awareness for projects – even before they technically exist.
- You may create some buzz around your project that will help you when it launches.
- It's exciting, and it's also a great way to expand your social connections.
- Whether successful or not, it provides an inexpensive learning experience – what you take away from the process will be subjective, but there's no question that such knowledge will apply to future projects and campaigns.

In a well-planned and -executed crowdfunding project, there aren't a lot of downsides, but there are always some risks you should be aware of too, however:

- You may fail to reach your goal (and be on the hook for any costs that your campaign has accrued). In almost all cases, however, you won't owe anything to the crowdfunding site or to backers in terms of rewards, as they will not be charged for their pledges.
- Your image may be tarnished by a project's failure to perform.
- Unsuccessful ventures may be seen as less viable when presented to potential future investors. You are unlikely to meet with success selling a project to prospective investors that has previously failed when presented through a crowdfunding campaign. The value of such ventures will be assumed to be greatly reduced.
- Supporting crowdfunding projects may consume more time, money and effort than you initially anticipated, or are prepared to invest.
- A fine line must be walked when promoting projects and asking for pledges – if you're not careful, you may annoy or distance potential allies.
- Your costs may be higher than anticipated, meaning that your goals may have been set too low or you didn't forecast expenses related to rewards, operations and overhead carefully.
- In a worst-case scenario, your project may get funded, but fail for other reasons. Understand that the legal issues surrounding failure to complete a project that has been crowdfunded, or one that arrives late or fails to meet expectations, are yet to be defined as well. Your liability in such situation may be hard to quantify, to say nothing of the personal sense of responsibility and obligation that you will feel to backers. Regardless of whatever legal complications may or may not occur, you will have to live with the knowledge that you let your community and backers down.
- If you're the sensitive type, realize that crowdfunding is the ultimate "putting yourself out there" experience. It's like being picked for the team in grade school. If you are chosen, you're happy and validated. If you aren't, or you're picked last, you feel rejected. Crowdfunding can trigger strong emotions, so be prepared.
- As with any form of solicitation, some friends, family and members of the general public may resent being asked for funds. However, while this is an inherent risk you will take

when crowdfunding, some negative response may be mitigated by your enthusiasm and positivity, and the perceived value and validity of your project.

## UNFORESEEN RISKS AND DRAWBACKS

Budgeting carefully and conservatively when planning crowdfunding projects is vital, as even the best-laid plans can go awry if funds are not accurately projected or mismanaged. Consider the case of software developer Warballoon Studios, who raised nearly $37,000 for its downloadable Android and iOS game, Star Command, for which it hoped to raise $20,000.

While the venture may appear to be successful, the company says far fewer funds than expected went into actual development, via a public post on its development blog to investors. Among the details revealed:

- Roughly $2000 of expected donations never materialized due to failed, reversed or rejected transactions – all of which added to the total featured on the game's project funding counter, but never actually hit the company's bank account.
- Fees from Kickstarter and Amazon totaled another $3000, siphoned from the project's overall tally before proceeds were received.
- Reward fulfillment cost the studio $10,000 alone, thanks to the expensive prizes used, with items offered in exchange for donations including printed posters, t-shirts, maps, MP3 samplers, and more. Warballoon says that had it budgeted again, it also would have included the costs to enlist help from a traditional product fulfillment house to handle the time and overhead associated with packaging and processing reward shipments.
- Around $6000 went to the composers who wrote the title's music.
- Poster design artwork cost the team $2000.
- Another $3000 was spent on buying a presence at trade show PAX East.
- Over $4000 was spent on lawyers, accountants and professional services, an expense the team says it wouldn't undertake again ("keep the attorneys out of it," they counsel).
- About $1000 was spent on iPad units required to test the game.
- As the tax year ended during the development cycle, another 30% of funds raised went to pay tax bills.
- As for the remaining $4000, it disappeared on daily costs and incidentals.

As you can see, even "success" is not without its perils – so be smart about your budgeting, operations and overhead. "All that said though," claims the team, "[the experience has] been great and the game would not be where it is if it wasn't for Kickstarter. We're extremely confident were going to hit our summer release date and that never would have happened without [our public backers]."

# Getting Your Crowdfunding Project Off of the Ground

People refer to crowdfunding projects as "campaigns," and they do so for a good reason. They require careful planning, clever resource allocation, consistent execution... and the recognition that even the best-laid plans may not survive initial contact with customers. You'll quickly discover that you are embarking upon a singularly time-consuming and challenging endeavor. Advance preparation is vital.

"Don't underestimate the amount of work [crowdfunding] campaigns require, both prior to and post launch," says Jordan Weisman (the driving force behind Shadowrun Returns on Kickstarter). "Just preparing a good video, taking time to make your message clear and editing the clip... to get the message across as intended takes a great deal of time. And then there's the written version of the story. The words are important. Look at which techniques have been successful for others and see how their methods apply to your project." Needless to say, his recommendations are just the tip of the iceberg.

## Pre-Launch Planning

As with campaigns of any kind, preparation is critical. Decisions made here can make or break your project, so don't rush into them. Take your time to do your research and get things right. Plan your campaign with care and forethought.

Points to keep in mind when planning a crowdfunding project include:

- Do your homework – Make sure that you have done your research on competitive products and campaigns, and understand precisely who and what you're going up against – as well as how your project can be positioned to differentiate itself and maximize its chances of success.
- Define and share a common goal – Everyone on the team should share a common vision of the project, be able to communicate a succinct description of its vision, understand who the venture's target audience is, and comprehend how to speak to this audience.
- Understand the stakes – If you are developing a new concept, product or IP, understand where the bar has been set by competing products and campaigns in terms of consumer expectation and production values. If you are leveraging an existing IP, fan base or market, research how many fans or customers exist for your venture, where to connect with them, and how they might consume information about it.

---

## HOW MUCH PLANNING TIME IS ENOUGH?

**"I spent three weeks preparing for our Kickstarter campaign. I stopped the com-
pany and that's all we focused on during this time. I also did a thorough analysis
of our budgets and reward tiers."**

-Brian Fargo, *Wasteland 2*

---

Now that you're in the right frame of mind in terms of project definition and focus, let's take
a look at what it takes to successfully build and execute a crowdfunding campaign around your
concepts.

# Preparing and Assessing Your Project

Your crowdfunding campaign is going to consist of several phases: Pre-launch preparation,
launch programs, post-launch management (and campaign evolution), and post-completion
follow-up. Each of these phases may require a considerable amount of work, especially if you are
successful. In fact, the more successful you are, the more work you can expect to do.

The pre-launch phase is critical. Planning is when you can make or break your project, so
don't rush into it. Take your time to do your homework and get things right.

1. **Study Other Projects**. This is critical. Look at campaigns that have worked and ones that
   have failed alike. What similarities and differences do they have with your project? What insights can you glean from them – and how can you avoid falling prey to the pitfalls on which
   they stumbled? Use this study time to also assess whether your project is really the kind of
   venture that works well in a crowdfunding environment, and what funding levels, rewards
   and marketing/social media campaigns are most appropriate.
2. **Prepare Assets in Advance**. Do you have enough product/project samples and supporting materials to quickly illustrate to potential backers what your idea is all about? Do
   you have visuals or videos that can clearly, quickly and concisely convey key message points,
   and demonstrate your project's upsides? If not, invest some time to develop corresponding images and/or videos that provide a clear impression of what your project is all about.
   A picture is worth a thousand words: Doubly so when you only have seconds to capture a
   viewer's attention.
3. **Perfect Your Pitch**. Refine your overarching vision and corresponding pitch, including all
   audiovisual and copywritten elements. Can you clearly and succinctly explain your project
   and its value in terms that your audience will understand and appreciate? Have you tried it
   out on friends and strangers to gauge their reaction and readjusted accordingly? Regardless
   of whether your project is ongoing or just beginning, or you've compiled pre-production

assets, do you have something to show potential backers? Do you have representative images or video to share that illustrate your project and supporting assets? What other audio-visual and copywritten elements (concept art, prototypes, sketches, in-development scenes, songs, etc) have you arranged to leverage? Perhaps you have notable individuals' testimonials to share or other kinds of support. Line up everything you can and plan how and when to use these materials. Be sure to plan a running promotional campaign that incorporates all elements – these materials will serve not only to define your project to the world, but as ammunition in the ongoing battle to promote it.

4. **Plan your Rewards**. Know what goods and services you have to offer, what they will cost you and how you will manufacture and distribute each. Be certain that you've created options that suit all pricing tiers, speak to a variety of backers, and have built in at least a handful or unique or eye-catching items and opportunities, if only for purposes of generating discussion.

5. **Project Budgeting and Completion**. Estimate how long it will take you to complete a project, allowing room for slippage – a 20-30% buffer is reasonable. Generate your budget and determine minimum funding levels (including any cushions) required to complete the project, and use a spreadsheet if necessary to calculate any costs that you may incur. Be sure to estimate service costs, expenses associated with reward fulfillment and even taxes (take time to speak with an accountant or other certified professional so that you fully understand potential financial and legal implications here) into your projected budget. Note that delays can have a significant effect on project overhead, shipping dates and funding goals.

6. **Funding Targets**. Don't make financial goals too high. Instead, ask for what you need at bare minimum to make a project work – and, in your project's description, describe added content, features, services or events that will be offered only if specific higher target goals are met. If you're successful, you may reach them. (Note that it's important to check funding rules for each individual site or service you are using before beginning as policies differ, i.e. most allow you to keep everything you make, even past your goal, but some do not.) Ultimately though, the less you're asking for, the likelier you are to incentivize potential backers into taking the plunge, as they'll be more willing to commit to goals that they believe are achievable.

7. **Campaign Duration**. Determine the optimum length of time to keep projects running. Some sites recommend that you keep the funding period down to as little as a few weeks, while others suggest that programs run for no more than 30 days at maximum. However, actual timeframes should be discussed and determined based on individual project need, including how much time it will take to raise awareness, how long you can sustain supporting promotional programs, and how important it is to create a sense of urgency (act now before funding closes!).

8. **Run a Systems Check**. Besides preparing campaign assets and tactics, ask yourself: Have you identified your target audience, and do you know where they consume news and media? Have you planned your reward strategies, and run them by friends and associates

to affirm that they appeal? Are you confident that your funding target is reasonable, and aimed low as possible to increase chances of success without compromising your budget? Have you identified PR, marketing, media and social media you will need create and utilize to reach your audience?

9. **Make Initial Outreach**. Try to drum up some initial interest from friends, family and colleagues, or any existing support base that you have, and secure their promise to contribute once campaigns initially start – their support and contributions may create a sense of successful forward momentum that spurs others to rally to the cause. Work hard to get momentum going around the project early, and ensure resources are ready to bring to bear on day one, before you officially launch it.

10. **Engage Fans Early**. If you have an existing fan base or strong group of potential supporters, engage them early – perhaps even weeks before launching your campaign. One way to do so is to solicit their opinions when determining which rewards you will offer. This is something that InXile founder Brian Fargo did with the *Wasteland 2* video game reboot project, and it helped catapult the venture forward from the moment it launched.

11. **Get Ready to Proceed**. Take a moment to pause, reflect and consider if you've set aside the time, funds and resources needed to dive in and make your crowdfunding campaign a success, and make sure that you are mentally and physically prepared to take the plunge. If so, it's time to put all your plans in motion, and begin generating some buzz.

## Insights from Campaigns that Failed

As many successful crowdfunding campaigns as there are out there, there are many times more that have failed. Having surveyed a large sampling, common characteristics shared by unsuccessful ventures appear to include:

### Lack of a trusted brand, brand identity, well-known personality, and/or lack of a compelling vision.

This is the most common reason that campaigns fail. Included in this category are also projects where the venture's overarching vision is left to the community to determine, rather than clearly defined by creators themselves. Likewise, if you fail to present backers with a credible personality that people can believe in who has a personal stake in the outcome, or launch projects without a large preexisting fan base or well-known brand attached, risks appear to be greatly magnified. Remember: Today's consumer is more skeptical than ever – building and maintaining trust and awareness is imperative.

### Failure to clearly explain and illustrate projects' core value proposition and/or benefits.

A number of historical campaigns have launched that have generated decent traffic and awareness, but ultimately secured little funding because consumers fundamentally failed to understand the service or opportunity being pitched, and/or its key benefits. Any project that generates frequent user questions asking you to clarify points or more clearly illustrate concepts in your introductory video is an immediate red flag. Happily, related issues can often be caught and addressed during pre-launch preparation phases by testing and screening campaign materials with objective observers (i.e. those who aren't team members and have no vested interest in the project) who can provide critical feedback.

## Lack of differentiation and the inability to define and communicate unique sales points.

Lack of differentiation is also a common project killer. Ask yourself: If you are pitching a book, film, game, television show, iPhone speaker dock or other product that looks and sounds like dozens of similarly-styled competitors, then why should anyone spend money on yours? Quickly and definitively finding ways to position your project uniquely and convey that uniqueness and value in your message is imperative. As a rule of thumb, at least one to three key selling points (the first tablet PC you can wirelessly connect to your TV, the only video game that lets you be the alien conqueror, a book you can read in the shower, etc.) should differentiate your project at a glance.

Bear in mind that these problems are especially pronounced in the entertainment, consumer products and video game fields, where themes and concepts are commonly recycled, and projects can take months to come to fruition. Case in point: If your new online virtual world looks similar to hundreds crowding the market, why should shoppers spend their hard-earned dollars on it at all, let alone now, when they won't get to play within it for months? Note that as more projects turn to crowdfunding solutions for backing, and consumers are given more choices about which products to back, competition will only become fiercer. As such, it's essential to immediately set yourself apart from the pack.

## Failure to generate awareness or engage potential backers.

Ever run across a great campaign and trailer from a project creator that's credible, unique, and completely worth paying attention to, but has failed to generate much in the way of donations? It may be suffering from a lack of consumer awareness, caused by insufficient or ineffectual PR, marketing and social media outreach. As a litmus test, run an online search on these campaigns' project names via Google and see: How many hits did you get? Then try searching for related news on Facebook, Twitter and other social media sites. Not coming up with much? You have a pretty clear idea of one major problem that's ailing the venture. On the flip side, you may stumble across campaigns that have generated tremendous media attention and conversation, but have also failed to translate that buzz into cold, hard cash. In this case, issues may be caused by poor pitch materials, a lack of ongoing campaign activity outside of an initial launch rush, lack of a viable product market, and/or an uninteresting or untenable reward structure.

## Setting campaign funding goals too high.

How much is too much? This is a tough question to answer, but it's wise to set your funding goal to the reasonable minimum required to deliver on your vision and no more. (Especially so as the more reasonable the figure, the likelier fans are to believe it's an achievable goal, and therefore the likelier they are to contribute.) Right-size products up-front by trimming designs back to the minimum number of options and features needed to deliver a high-quality and compelling value proposition, thereby scissoring out extraneous additions and needless expenses. However, you should always estimate conservatively and provide some cushion in your budget in case of scheduling slips, distribution issues, and other unforeseen mishaps.

Once done, take a hard look at how many potential backers there might be out there for your project. As a simple starting point, it may help to consider: How many are posting in your online forums or those of websites related to similar topics? Estimate conservatively, and consider how many might actively contribute (again, remember that it may be a very small percentage of the overall target market), and decide if you need to rework your project's scope and revise budgets and projections accordingly. Case in point: Millions of users may have fond memories of game designer Tim Schafer's classic adventures, over 87,000 of whom contributed to his Kickstarter campaign. But while Schafer was able to attract more backers to the venture than any project in history, even that number of converted fans was just a small percentage of his potential target audience.

So be realistic about how many potential backers may exist for a given venture, how many you can reach, how many you can convince to give you money, and how much, on average, contributors will spend. If you do the math, and the numbers add up, you'll stand a much better chance of meeting funding goals.

# Creating an Effective Pitch

Your pitch is your first point of contact with potential backers, and opening salvo in the war to win their hearts and minds – and you know what they say about first impressions. Note that an effective pitch requires exhaustive preparation and execution. Don't wing it. Plan it. Work it. Refine it. Test it on unsuspecting friends. Solicit feedback. Play devil's advocate, and consider everything that can go wrong. Tweak, pull and modify it until you're certain it can't be better. In other words, you've only got one chance to make a successful debut: Make sure it's the best pitch you can offer.

Your pitch will consist primarily of two components: A video and a written introduction to your project.

## The Video Pitch

The video pitch can be one of the most persuasive and effective tools that project builders have to engage an audience and potential backers. Here are some ground rules for effective video pitches:

1. Start by examining at least 10 other video pitches before beginning. Look at successful projects and unsuccessful ones alike. Think about and analyze why some were better than others and plan your video accordingly.
2. Next, prepare – and then prepare some more. Make sure you have something eye-catching to show that will quickly grab people's attention and make them interested in your project.
3. Keep the contents of your video short, simple and engaging: You should grab the viewer's attention in the first 10 seconds and keep things brisk and engaging – upwards of two minutes is pushing it for overall length, given shortened online attention spans.
4. Make sure your pitch clearly demonstrates your project, key selling points and what makes it unique. Videos should clearly represent each new venture and why it's so original and compelling. Let viewers know: Why are you passionate about projects, and why should they be as well?
5. Clips don't have to be "professional" or polished. However, you must make sure that segments aren't choppy, poorly lit or difficult to discern, and that audio is clear and understandable.
6. Be yourself – and be natural and upbeat. You want people to believe in you, to be on your side, and to want your project to succeed. Remember, you're selling yourself as much as you're selling the project. Bear in mind, however: You're not a used car salesman or a discount furniture wholesaler – honesty and warmth are essential. You can be nerdy or funny or even a little awkward. It's OK, as long as you're authentic, and express yourself clearly and with genuine enthusiasm.

7.  Rehearse your pitch so that it becomes second nature. Learn to express yourself concisely and with a positive and enthusiastic attitude. Remember, you are your project's biggest evangelist – if people don't think that you believe in the venture, they won't either.

8.  Describe your project, your goals, why you need the money, how you'll use it and the time frame in which you need pledges to come in. And definitely don't forget to describe the rewards you have to offer. Answer these questions for the audience:

    - Who are you?
    - What is your background relevant to this project? Why should I trust you?
    - What is your project?
    - What's so special about it?
    - What does it look like?
    - How long will it take to complete the project?
    - How much backing do you need to complete the project?
    - How will you use the money?
    - What rewards are you offering?
    - What will you do if you get more money than you are asking for?
    - Why is your project worth viewers' hard-earned dollars?
    - How will you keep in touch with the community during development, and after the product is released?

Be reasonable. Only promise content, features, services or opportunities that you know you will be able to deliver upon if goals are met. Save inessential or riskier additions for updates and "stretch goals" that can be added once your initial goal is achieved. (Note that it's important to check funding rules on the site or services you are using before beginning… most allow you to keep everything you make, even past your goal, but some do not.) It is also important to check rules regarding copyrighted content. If you don't own it or make it yourself, be sure that you have the rights to use it.

---

## CONNECTING WITH CONTRIBUTORS

**"If you don't come in with a known reputation, you have to build it and present a good representation of what it is that you want to make. Be yourself. Just like traditional investors, backers are investing in people. Keep your pitch short. Tell your story concisely and avoid being overly filled with angst. Your goal is to inspire potential backers. Be clear about the scope of what it is that you're doing and convince your audience of your belief in your ability to pull it off."**

-Jordan Weisman, *Shadowrun Returns*

# CREATING POWERFUL ONLINE VIDEOS

Once upon a time, video production was the sole province of broadcast professionals. Nowadays, it's accessible to lone individuals working out of a spare bedroom or garage. Happily for crowdfunding enthusiasts, assembling eye-catching clips doesn't have to cost a small fortune or even require hiring a dedicated cameraman. Following is everything you need to know to design and build an effective video pitch.

1. **Choose the Right Hardware** – While you'll still get the best results from a proper video camera (see: models by Samsung, Canon, Panasonic, etc.), pocket camcorders can all produce perfectly Web-worthy results too. Sony's Bloggie 3D even lets you shoot in full 3D for under $200, while the iPhone 4 offers 1080p HD filming right from your pocket. Whichever route you choose, pick a model that shoots in 720p high-definition (HD) minimum, and offers external microphone input. Ideally, you'll want a unit that supports expandable SD memory cards or external storage as well. It's also important to go hands-on with all options before buying to gauge the capability of extras such as low-light filming performance, image stabilization, color reproduction, clarity, and battery life. Pro tip: If illumination is an issue, try picking up some clamp lights at Home Depot – likewise, external microphones (especially clip-ons) can make a huge difference in production values.

2. **Pick Your Battles** – Cute is good, but clear and concise is better – so keep it simple, but engaging. Before filming your first frame, make certain you've got a clear idea of the topic you'd like to cover, and determine the conceptual angle you'll take to differentiate your viewpoint from the thousands already cluttering up cyberspace. Also consider what tone and form the video should take: Behind-the-scenes documentary, comedic skit, etc. The options here are infinite, offering little excuse to skimp on originality. To succeed with video pitches, though, remember this: You need to take a singular, unique approach that instantly makes your ideas pop off the screen and be memorable to viewers as a result.

3. **Take a Stance** – Video's greatest strength is arguably the sense of empathy and familiarity that the medium creates between viewers and on-screen talent. So don't be coy – get out there and make your opinion heard. This doesn't mean that you have to be obnoxious: Just engaging enough to catch someone's eye, and convey your singular sense of personality. Pitches are most effective when you can establish a unique point of view and perspective. Positive, negative, completely off the wall... pick an approach and run with it. After all, why should anyone bother tuning in if you're not speaking up and saying something of interest?

4. **Grab Viewers' Attention** – Audiences' spare time is shorter, and their attention spans are more divided than ever – especially when it comes to a sales pitch. So if you can't excite or engage them in the first 5-15 seconds, it's time to rethink your approach. The opening moments of any video should be brisk, arresting and straight to the point, explaining your project and its unique attributes up-front. Go big or go home right off the bat, and don't ignore

the importance of maintaining a sense of pacing or excitement – failing to sustain momentum can lead to viewer attrition. Shorter clips (90 seconds to 2-3 minutes max is an ideal length for short-form Web content and crowdfunding pitches) work best. Note that the key is always to say more with less, be it pictures, animations, diagrams, or jaw-dropping b-roll.

5. **Don't Overdo It** – You don't need glossy production values, high-concept sets or fancy editing tricks to engage audiences on the Web, where a rawer, more organic form of dialogue is encouraged. That doesn't mean you should skimp on quality – nothing alienates viewers quicker than poor audio, bad lighting or endless technical hiccups. Rather, scenarios and subjects should seem compelling and delivered in a plausible context. Likewise, dialogue should feel casual and off-the-cuff – the same way it would when talking to friends, colleagues or associates in real life. Ultimately, you're trying to package and present a compelling story that speaks to others in a language they can understand. Unless they're key selling points of your project, that doesn't mean having to dress everything up with fancy scripts, snazzy animations or mind-blowing 3D special effects.

6. **Keep the Message Simple** – Too many video campaigns, even multimillion-dollar Super Bowl ads, forget the cardinal rule: Keep it simple, stupid. It pays to establish very quickly off the bat what the core point(s) are that you're trying to make. Subsequent imagery and commentary, though informative and entertaining where appropriate, should simply serve to reinforce these highlights. An easy way to stay on track: Pick one to three key bullet points you'd like to get across before beginning, and use them as a guidepost throughout production. Just be careful not to err too much on the side of repetition, which gets monotonous, or lean too heavily on surprise, humor or excitement at the expense of clarity.

7. **Focus on Value Creation** – If you're going to ask someone for a chunk of their time or, tougher still, to actively reach into their wallet, you must offer something of meaningful value as part of the trade-off. Simple ways to do so when pitching crowdfunded campaigns include, but aren't limited to, eye-catching product demonstrations, commentary by famed individuals, and compelling insights on how your ventures put a completely new spin on the status quo. Consider what has real, tangible value to your viewer, and provide it – only then have you earned the right to ask for something in return.

8. **Don't Be Afraid to Laugh** – Transparency can be a tricky subject for many businesses keen to promote a particular product or service. Push a project too overtly, and viewers tune it out. Take too soft an approach with sales pitches and you risk them not making the connection or feeling compelled to take action. Sometimes, breaking the fourth wall and either speaking directly to the viewer or letting them know you're aware of the irony of the situation can help bridge the gap. Just be careful to use the technique sparingly, as it won't fit all scenarios, and don't lean too self-ironic, or you risk damaging the credibility of yourself and your wares.

9. **Include a Call to Action** – Any video can act as a simple branding exercise, serving to raise the profile of your projects. But those intended to generate a measurable audience reaction need to ask viewers to take an actionable step in order to generate one. This call

to action can take the form of a simple request ("donate by Friday to receive an exclusive reward"), solicitation of viewer feedback ("email us your best ideas for the launch party here") or any number of alternatives. The lesson here: Creativity pays, but interactivity is more important still – if you want to derive real value from your videos and spur donors to action, repeat as follows: Passivity is a thing of the past.

10. **Spread the Word** – Videos, like crowdfunded campaigns themselves, can certainly snowball through word-of-mouth channels. But to get to that point, they first need to reach critical mass. Make sure you get the word out about them to aid in viewer discovery. All clips you create should be not only readily embeddable on blogs and web pages, but also fully supported via press releases, social media mentions and other marketing and public relations tools that help generate excitement, and drum up interest in your campaigns.

Excerpted from The Business Expert's Guidebook
(free to download at www.ASmallBusinessExpert.com).

For examples of successful online videos, see below:

# HOW TO IMPROVE YOUR CHANCES OF GETTING FUNDED

**A few of us [well-known game designers], like Tim Schafer, Brian Fargo and I, have a known reputation and our projects already have many fans. That is an advantage we have, but even if you don't have that reputation, you can still establish yourself and inspire potential backers.**

**Put a lot of sweat equity into a project before you even begin. Make sure you have something to show that is really going to present a beautiful example of what you're going to do. A good example is what the developers of The Banner Saga did. They worked hard before they launched their Kickstarter campaign, and it showed.**

**Finally, be yourself – like traditional investors, backers are investing in people – and describe the scope of what you're doing in your project. Help people believe that you can pull it off.**

- Jordan Weisman, *Shadowrun Returns*

## PERFECTING YOUR PITCH

Noted designer Tim Schafer and his development studio, Double Fine, recently turned heads by raising over $3.3 million dollars for a new interactive adventure (over 10x more than was being asked for) that established game publishers wouldn't touch with a 10-foot pole. Per a recent interview with IndieDB.com, this wasn't just by serendipity, according to the cult icon: He and his cohorts did so by convincing the world that this project was a meaningful event – and a time-sensitive one that backers had to be an indelible part of, or risk losing the opportunity forever. Want to convince potential contributors that they need to hop on the proverbial train before it leaves the station as well? Apart from remembering the golden rule ("a good pitch is a good story," he says), here's the advice Schafer provides for creating your own sense of interest and urgency around projects. And, of course, a pitch convincing enough that it inspires fans to dip into their wallets.

1. **Make a convincing case** – Provide a clear-cut and persuasive argument why projects matter, including offering a succinct explanation of the unique opportunity that exists, why

you're the person/team team to do it, and why the moment to strike is now – and do so decisively at that. If possible, involve fans throughout the development process to create greater resonance and emotional investment.

2. **Validate your approach** – Explain what makes your approach singular and successful – and why fans can't afford to let the opportunity pass. Let backers know why this isn't just a project, but rather a movement or unique moment in history, and one they can't afford to let go by the wayside. Help them see and share your vision, and where it has the potential to go.

3. **Certify your credentials** – Prove to fans that you and your team bring something unique and/or irreplaceable to the table – and therefore are the right ones to bring the vision to life in a way that simply can't be replicated elsewhere. From singular skill sets to the involvement of well-known and beloved personalities, help contributors understand why you're the best men or women for the job.

4. **Show that time is ticking** – Build a strong call to action into campaigns by creating a sense of urgency around them. Illustrate why the time to act is now and why there's pressing reason to rally to the cause before it's too late.

5. **Transcend from project to movement** – Go beyond promoting simple projects and products to give fans a glimpse at the bigger picture, and demonstrate how their support can make monumental events happen. Embrace your backers, and make them a part of the conversation. Solicit fan feedback, offer tangible value in return for contributors' time and money, and – most of all – make an active point of taking sponsors along on an once-in-a-lifetime journey where you steer the ship, but they too experience every twist and turn on the ride.

Important to consider as well: Schafer also advises uses personalized, premium rewards for your biggest financial backers and fans – the more custom-tailored or opportunities for end-user involvement each provides, the better. If you can bring all these elements together, not only will you have a convincing pitch, in his mind. You'll also have a chance at beating what the celebrated designer still views as considerably long odds, and – more importantly – the potential makings of something special on your hands.

## The Project Homepage

Your video is important, but before potential backers even view it, they'll first land on your campaign's homepage to find out more about your project. Part of what will drive traffic there, and prompt them to learn more and consider financial contributions, is the brief summary and image that people will see when they initially browse your chosen crowdfunding service/site. Bearing this in mind, be sure you can describe your vision for the project concisely and that you have a good snapshot to accompany it, which will often be a still image from your video pitch.

Once prospective patrons have arrived at your homepage, you will want to grab their attention quickly and explain what your project is, what makes it unique and why they'd want to invest in the venture. Naturally, you should carefully think through everything you are going to put on the page. Here are some suggestions:

- **Do Your Research**. Just as when putting together campaign videos, it's important to assess and review several examples of pitch pages for both successful and unsuccessful projects. Note what you like about them and which elements grab your attention. From off-putting aesthetic designs to dense text descriptions, take note of which aspects of these pages don't seem to work as well. Take these findings into account, and plan your homepage, pitch and supporting assets accordingly.
- **Create Compelling Headlines**. Bold callouts that break up text descriptions into easily digestible sections not only give people an idea of the subject matter contained within each grouping, helping to make descriptions more approachable and alleviate monotony. They also adorn them with naturally eye-catching headers. For online reading, remember: Short, simple write-ups work best, with longer clips more effective when subdivided into more user-friendly nuggets, which also serve the added benefit of more capably attracting viewers' attention.
- **Use Arresting Images**. Eye-catching pictures and screenshots that represent your project do wonders for your home page. Try to find several attractive photos that showcase your project and possibly the people behind it as well. Note that wherever possible, all should speak to and communicate one or more of the three key ideas and messages you're trying to get across. In fact, using photos to convey these points can be much quicker and more effective, and provide the advantage of helping you say less with fewer words. Keep in mind that action shots are frequently more effective than stills as well.
- **Leverage Notable Personalities**. If you can get people from outside your project to recommend it – particularly those with a strong following whom your target audience would trust and believe – use their commentary wherever possible to reinforce your message. Likewise, where suitable, consider inserting a very short video of a noteworthy individual or someone credible that supports your project explaining why they believe in it.
- **Write Attention-Getting Descriptions**. What you write about your project and how you describe it is very important. People will read it and want to find that all of their key questions have been answered. At minimum, here is what you need to tell them:

  - Who are you?
  - What is your background relevant to this project?
  - Why should I trust you?
  - What is your project?
  - What's so special or unique about it?
  - What does it look like?
  - How long will it take to complete the project?

- How much backing do you need to complete the project?
- How will you use the money?
- What rewards are you offering?
- What will you do if you get more money than you are asking for?
- Why is your project worth readers' hard-earned dollars?
- How will you keep in touch with the community during development, and after the product is released?

## THE IMPORTANCE OF KEEPING IT SIMPLE

**"People told us that our message was too complicated. We learned that we needed to simplify, and make the message more basic [to communicate better with fans.]"**

- Jane Jensen, *Pinkerton Road: A Year of Adventure*

## Building Effective Rewards

If you try to launch a crowdfunding project by just asking for contributions and not offering anything of tangible value in return, you'll very quickly discover that crowdfunding isn't like running a political campaign or charity fundraiser. Few people will give you money just because they like your project. Some generous souls might, but the majority of people you want to attract expect something in return – hence the need to incentivize potential backers by offering goods or services in return for their contributions.

In the case of physical goods, the notion of pre-ordering, or placing an advance payment with a retailer in return for reservations (and possibly exclusive rewards) now, and then a copy of the product or creative work when it eventually releases, is a well-established practice. Similar transactions work well under the crowdfunding model, especially when coupled with eye-catching or exclusive extras. From elaborate "Collector's Editions" – e.g. lavish DVD packaging and bonus content for high-level backers of what might otherwise be a digitally distributed film – to limited edition coffee table books or director's cut videos, myriad options present themselves.

The type of reward you offer is, to some extent, determined by the kind of project you're running. In the case of special events, for instance, you might offer free admission, better seating, backstage passes, or even a chance to hop up onstage and jam with a favorite band. For consumer products, the first and most obvious reward would be to provide backers with a digital or physical copy of the item in advance and/or at a price far less than the typical retail value. From there, you can tack on or bundle together other rewards. Bear in mind that creativity pays, however, and that not all rewards have to involve the exchange of physical goods. Many of the most popular rewards with contributors often include personal or unique touches, or are based around singular opportunities, e.g. lunch with a famed musician, a personal appearance on their album, or the chance to play backing guitar for them at a recording session.

A multitude of rewards and inducements for patronage have been shown to be effective, and with possibilities ultimately as endless as the variety of campaigns themselves, more continue to evolve every day.

---

## IMPROVING AND ENHANCING REWARDS

**"Once thing we realized as we reviewed our campaign and looked at our pricing tiers was that we could improve them, and really tried to understand the psychology of tiers. Initially, we made over $30,000 through sales of our $15 tier rewards, and only $4000 via our $30 tier ones, so we changed them to be more attractive and added an extra copy of the game. We also added new rewards, such as a novella by Chris Avellone, and a video blog. The moves paid off."**

-Brian Fargo, *Wasteland 2*

---

## Sample Rewards

When weighing reward prospects, be sure to research similar projects to see what type of rewards have been provided previously, what strategies worked and didn't, overall distribution makeup of reward structures, and individual items' and package deals' respective contributions to campaigns' bottom line. Following are examples of some of the kinds of rewards that you might consider offering:

- **The product itself**. Be sure to calculate any costs associated with this kind of reward and figure them into your pricing structure and funding goals. If working with outside vendors, be aware that there may be distribution costs or limitations that strategic partners will impose regarding the number and variety of items that you can discount and use as rewards.
- **Advanced or early access to the product or preproduction units**. Or, for that matter, alpha and beta testing programs.
- **Enhanced versions of the product**. For instance, autographed, deluxe, director's cut and collector's editions.
- **Merchandise and souvenirs**. Besides "making of" books and autographed materials, you might offer posters, stickers, t-shirts, caps and other items that commemorate the project.
- **Behind-the-scenes photos, videos and booklets**. Items that show the people, con-

cept work and other elements featured within the project – especially if there is a large visual component to it.

- **Opportunities to affect the project's eventual outcome**. Some film, book, music, TV, theater and video game projects allow backers at certain levels to suggest how stories develop, what's included in the finished package, and featured subjects or locations. Be advised, however: Caution should be taken here so as not to leave potential backers with the impression that the overall product vision is unfocused, not clear, or subject to significant change. A number of campaigns have failed when concepts were left up entirely to the online community to define, potentially because consumers had less confidence in a product whose vision was TBD.

- **Making your backers part of the product**. Some creative projects allow backers at certain levels to be a character within the narrative, soundtrack or action itself.

- **Giving contributors credit**. It's always a good idea to thank your backers, but sometimes there are ways to do so publicly, within the product itself (ex. within the liner notes, or book or game credits) or at surrounding events via mentions over a microphone or banners/signs specifically thanking especially generous donors.

- **Combined rewards**. Rewards that combine several other rewards into one, or bundle several pricing tiers worth of incentives' together. Many successful campaigns use an "all of the above" strategy, offering simple rewards at lower tiers and then simply adding new offers on top of them, so that most tiers begin with "all previous rewards plus…"

- **Exclusive access**. Chances to meet people who are part of the creative team behind various projects, or related notables (e.g. actors, directors, musicians, artists, online celebrities, etc.) whom audiences would like a chance to interact with.

- **Private parties, events and occasions.** Some projects offer special events as a reward to donors – usually the ones at the highest tiers. Rewards might include invitations to exclusive launch parties, private events held in backers' honor or grand gala affairs that will be held if the project earns certain dollar amounts above and beyond its initial goal.

There are lots of options when it comes to creating unique, eye-catching and memorable rewards. Pick the ones that fit your project best.

# LISTEN TO YOUR FANS

"[When building reward tiers], we looked at what other people had done, and I created an Excel spreadsheet to figure our costs to make sure we weren't spending more than what we were making. I made a lot of adjustments, and we also edited and added new tiers after we went live. For instance, we discovered that people really wanted memorabilia from past games and boxed versions of titles. Listening to what people were saying and asking for was crucial."

- Jane Jensen, *Pinkerton Road: A Year of Adventure*

## Reward Levels

Each reward that you create will be associated with a specific monetary donation amount referred to as a "tier." For instance, in exchange for donations made at the $15 pricing tier, you might offer a digital copy of your game or a PDF version of your book. For $30, you might instead offer a boxed copy of the game or a printed edition of the book instead. The trick is to structure rewards so that there are options for donors who wish to contribute at all tiers, without huge gaps between them. Case in point: You don't want the next funding level up from a $10 reward to cost $1000, as you'd risk alienating many potential contributors.

Note that while it's OK to have some lower pledge tiers that don't include a physical reward, it's always best to have some tangible benefit tied to every tier. Also, keep in mind that backers often do have the option to pledge without expecting a reward in exchange for contributions. For instance, on Kickstarter, backers can check an option that says they don't need anything in exchange for their donation.

At the top of your reward tier structure, you should offer very special incentives, including unique, one-of-a-kind opportunities and experiences. What kinds of offers you make will, again, depend on your project and what you have to offer. Examples might include a personal guided tour of your studio with a gourmet lunch, or chance to meet and chat with one of today's greatest film directors about their creative direction for a motion picture, perhaps. With the possibility of changes to U.S. law, it may even become possible to offer equity in your company or project, though this is not presently allowed at the time of this writing.

## CREATING SUCCESSFUL REWARDS

"We found our most successful rewards to be simply the game itself as well as the book of art. However, [exclusive or specialized rewards] can also do very well. As an example, we offered three very special $10,000 donation tiers [with accompanying rewards] and they also sold out."

- Jordan Weisman, *Shadowrun Returns*

## Final Check

Before you hit the launch button, carefully go through and review everything you've compiled thus far carefully. Double-check your video pitch and make sure it's correctly paced; toned and gets the point across; be certain that rewards make sense, are attention-getting and are appropriately priced; and ensure that your homepage pitch and supporting assets are all first-rate. Never settle for "good enough." Your video and project home page speak volumes, and will ultimately determine how you will be judged – don't skimp on presentation, and be certain that they clearly and effectively depict the message and image that you want them to project.

Get other people to give you their feedback, too. Not just your friends and family, but if possible, individuals you trust to provide an objective – and, if needed, harsh – opinion. Several crowdfunding sites allow you to share links to the pre-launch version of your site: Take the opportunity to solicit feedback and support from associates and partners who will be assisting you with the campaign. While you can make changes after you launch, it should be a last resort, given the public nature of these updates.

Again, take a moment to review your reward structure. Be sure that it contains attractive and compelling options, offers a variety of pricing tiers and options for all budgets, and that there are no hidden costs to come back and bite you. Keep in mind any fees associated with maintaining operations and added expenses, and realize that unless you are a non-profit, you will pay taxes on the money you receive from your crowdfunding campaign.

Also make sure that you comply with the rules of the site you are using, and all corresponding professional and financial obligations. Note that most prohibit you from using copyrighted material for which you do not have permission. Make sure you are compliant on all fronts. Vital as well from a legal standpoint: If project responsibility relies with a business, not individuals, make sure details of company incorporation and formation are settled in advance, and that ownership of intellectual property (IP) rights are clearly defined before debuting.

Make sure that you have assembled a community of fans, friends, and partners who will jump on the site the moment it is launched, register and commit, and then spread the word via social networks. At minimum, do you have a Facebook page, Google+ account, Pinterest profile and YouTube feed setup? Does everybody know what Twitter account and hashtag to use?

Worth asking yourself as well: Is your marketing plan in place? Are assets lined up and ready to go for the duration of your campaign, so you're not scrambling at the last minute? Have you created a standalone project website, separate from that which exists on crowdfunding platforms, to direct searches and fan activity to as well? Did you secure support from friends and family, who can rally to the cause and cause an initial avalanche of activity? Have you lined up initial media support and buzz?

Once you press the launch button, you are committed.

You want to be generating a marked response in order to get the ball rolling and to spread the word virally. If you have a truly unique project or any press contacts, try to secure coverage for your project in advance (no more than two weeks prior to announcement due to journalists' increasingly busy schedules, however). See if you can arrange for stories to hit at or around the time you launch to raise your profile and create the impression of success – but don't think that the odd mention here or there will be enough. Try to plan PR campaigns so that you generate an initial groundswell of buzz and appear to be everywhere at once, but then roll out attention-getting activities at different intervals during your crowdfunding campaign to sustain awareness. The trick is to keep the conversation with the public growing and never let it die out. Note that if you've never created or run a PR or marketing campaign before, and are unsure of your ability to raise awareness or generate interest, a modest investment in professional help may be advised.

Everything ready to go? Then go ahead and take the plunge: Press that button and get ready for the next phase of the campaign. We're just getting started.

## PLOTTING YOUR PUBLIC RELATIONS CAMPAIGN

"[For public relations and media outreach], we hired a PR person with great connections in the adventure genre, and she was very helpful. We also started working on Facebook a little late, but we got a lot of responses. That said, keeping up with it all was a full-time job."

- Jane Jensen, *Pinkerton Road: A Year of Adventure*

"In our case, we were able to reach out to journalists and editors who had a passion for the property. They responded with exposure to their readership. We also had the advantage of being able to leverage existing fan groups. Some of these activities map well against launching new intellectual properties as well. If you have a highly-identified player demographic, go where they live and start talking to them – even in advance of launch."

-Jordan Weisman, *Shadowrun Returns*

## WHEN SHOULD YOU LAUNCH?

"One big mistake we made was launching on a Tuesday at 5AM. When you launch determines when your project ends. Maybe it would have been better set at another day and time, like 5PM on a Friday. We could have had a great final day and a closing party. We could also have promoted that last opportunity to pledge... those final hours. But not on a Tuesday at 5AM."

-Brian Fargo, *Wasteland 2*

# After Launch, What Now?

The minute you launch your crowdfunding campaign, the clock starts ticking. If you've prepared well in advance, you should have a small (or large) army of friends and supporters rushing to be the first to respond and, at the same time, help spread the word through traditional and social media contacts.

But such activities are just the beginning. Now the real legwork associated with any campaign begins, because launching the project is just the opening gun – you've still got a proverbial marathon to run. Your core task now isn't just to keep chatter surrounding your project alive – it's to sustain and nurture that buzz, ultimately serving to make it grow even bigger. Not a day should go by that you (and your friends and partners) aren't updating, tweeting, posting news, calling on prospective patrons, handing out promotional cards, or any combination of the above in order to help promote your project.

Don't forget to acknowledge your backers either – and do so soon and often. It's imperative to maintain a running dialogue with them through direct messages and mass updates. If you've kept some really special and engaging rewards under wraps prior to launch, now's the time to begin trotting them out at regular intervals, to establish a running cadence. Pick regular times to add them to the queue and update sites with news of them all as well. (This helps remind users when to keep coming back to receive new updates.) Then send an announcement out to let everyone know. Keep thinking of ways to keep the project fresh and alive in your audience's mind – the squeaky wheel gets the grease.

Answer all questions immediately, and address any concerns or potential problems raised by your backers. Make changes as needed and always – we repeat, always – stay current and up to date in your conversations with contributors. They are lifeblood of your campaign.

---

## MAKING A COMMITMENT TO YOUR BACKERS

**"You launch and then there's a very large commitment in terms of responsiveness that's required… It's vital to answer questions, stay active on comment forums and provide running updates. Keep up with personal correspondence. Keep up with questions. You have to be mentally prepared for that."**
- Jordan Weisman, *Shadowrun Returns*

---

Some people maintain a blog where they continue to share information about the project and other news and material of interest to their audience. Whichever your preferred method for staying connected with fans, the mandate is simple: Keep them riveted. If you can, continue to entertain your audience with behind-the-scenes peeks, project updates and stories told through posts and videos, cool new concept art, or any other vehicle that engages them. Likewise, it may also pay dividends (both figuratively and literally) to solicit your backers' involvement in some of the decision making – and most certainly will to include them in the conversation. Have no doubt that a lot of contributors will be happy to share their ideas for making your campaign more successful – solicited or not. After all, who more than they wants to see you succeed?

## THE NEW SHAPE OF CUSTOMER SERVICE

"It's hard to imagine the sheer amount of fan reactions and things flying our way that we were unprepared for. We would check our PR inbox to find 1500 messages waiting. There were so many questions that the sheer amount paralyzed us. But we answered every question, just not all press requests. Even now we have all these people asking questions or contacting us because their credit card maxed out or was canceled. With 61,000 backers, we're also dealing with thousands of issues – legitimate ones at that. We have to deal with all of them."

-Brian Fargo, *Wasteland 2*

## Marketing and Advertising

One thing that's important to keep in mind is that every crowdfunding campaign is, at heart, essentially a consumer marketing effort. If people don't know about your project, there's no way they can contribute to it. And the primary way we as project creators have to raise awareness amongst large groups of people is through marketing, whether through social media, public relations or more traditional promotional channels.

So far, traditional advertising vehicles – e.g. paid advertisements – haven't been a major element of crowdfunding ventures. But it's entirely plausible that they may soon be used effectively as an element of a successful campaign strategy. However, be advised: It has been shown time and again that social media can be a highly effective substitute. Moreover, while positive press mentions may generate occasional spikes in traffic and donations, a running combination of press and social media activities can be even more effective. Even if you're not normally an active social media user, it literally pays to become one when pursuing crowdfunding ventures – if you can get even a few friends to help disseminate your message, it has the potential to grow like wildfire. Along similar lines, if you can get even one mention in a blog or newspaper or other major media outlet, it might spur additional interest. (The other, and sometimes more likely, effect of such stories is to cement credibility and provide grist for the promotional mill, providing an easily shareable reference that may help to better explain or call attention to your project.) Ultimately, the key when it comes to marketing a crowdfunding project is to create a constant stream of dialogue that steadily increases in volume to an eventual crescendo. If you are successful at lighting the initial spark, and continue to stoke the fire, the message will continue to spread.

Twitter is an especially effective vehicle for promoting news and announcements surrounding crowdfunded campaigns. Information and ideas can spread through the Twitterverse at the speed of light – if you can gain some traction. One way to kickstart interest: If you know people who are influential in your field, follow them on Twitter and engage in some of their conversations, finding opportunities to mention your project where it's polite and makes sense. Or – better yet – get them involved in the venture and ask them for help marshalling their user base by sharing details of their involvement. (Example: If a famed personality writes your new book's foreword, appears in your documentary or offers a private dinner and conversation as a reward for high-level contributors, perhaps they wouldn't mind sharing details with fans via blogs, Facebook updates and other online postings.) Of course, other forms of social media, such as Facebook, LinkedIn, BranchedOut, Google+ and any other networks to which you belong may also provide effective ways to get the word out. Groups and communities – in the real world or virtual – are always great places to start.

Worth remembering: There are a lot of tools you can use to automate your social outreach. The apps, programs and services below all allow you to send messages to multiple social media sites, including Twitter, Facebook and other popular choices, and they also let you schedule messages to post at prime times when your audience will be watching. Like certain choices below, many other solutions may also be available as a free or paid download on mobile devices such as phones and tablet PCs.

Hootsuite
Tweetdeck
SproutSocial
SocialOomph

Industry events and conventions, if they coincide with the dates of your crowdsourcing campaign, are also ideal places to build buzz. Print up promotional cards with information about your project and hand them out to everybody you meet, or circulate them throughout the press room and gift bags as organizers permit. Take advantage of opportunities to speak on panels or provide bylined articles for industry gatherings and trade publications, and otherwise do everything you can to talk the venture up, in person and online, whenever possible.

Consider yourself shy? Get over it, Poindexter. All joking aside, while you can revert to being soft-spoken again in a few weeks, while your campaign is running, you cannot afford to be coy – and, in fact, need to be social to the Nth degree. As the face of, and lead cheerleader for, your crowfunding campaign, it's vital that you be visible, active and something of a lightning rod – the more attention you can bring to your projects, the more funding you'll potentially raise and the farther word may eventually spread. If being the face of the campaign just isn't in your DNA, perhaps there is someone else on your team better suited to the task. Don't be ashamed to cede this responsibility to an associate whose skill set better fits the task at hand.

Success is simple: You need constant contact with the social universe and with your backers, and a running stream of things to say of merit in order to keep the conversation going. Never, ever let a day go by where you didn't reach out to your existing audience, or prospective backers, in a multitude of ways.

## Campaign Completed – What's Next?

Succeed or fail, you may think your work is over once the project reaches its end, but that would be a mistake. Sure, you can breathe a big sigh of relief that you've succeeded, or lick your wounds and get started planning your next campaign if not, but it's definitely not time to walk away from your backers and your campaign. First, some crucial fan-creator interactions still have to happen.

### Say Thank You

Not surprisingly, the first order of business is to thank all your backers profusely. The more personally you can do this, the better. A project update is one way. A personal message to each of them is even better. If you have kept up all along with comments and private messages, you have established a connection with your backers, which promotes both gratitude and trust. You know how much they want you to succeed – reciprocate their enthusiasm by showing just how grateful and enthusiastic you are about their support.

### Collect Information

Next, you will need to assess the rewards you've offered and make sure you can fulfill them. What do you need to know from your backers in order to fulfill their pledges? In many cases you'll need their physical addresses for rewards that require mailing. You probably already have their names and email addresses, which are generally included with the list of people who have pledged.

We strongly recommend that you create your own database or spreadsheet containing details on all your backers, including how much they pledged and which rewards they chose. This is especially important if you cannot fulfill rewards immediately, which would be the case if you were creating a product or venture that cannot be completed for some time. In the case of a major undertaking such as developing a book, movie or video game, final delivery could take many months or even over a year to occur due to the time-consuming process of development and post-production. Thankfully, most crowdfunding sites offer tools that can help you gather contributors' information, including surveys that you can design and send out to make the data collection process simpler.

## Stay Connected

Finally, maintain running contact with your backers. They are enthusiastic about your project. Keep them involved. Some people setup an ongoing blog with regular updates and even an inside look at their project as it evolves. Not only does it show respect and gratitude: It can also provide a rare glimpse into what for many fans is an arcane and mysterious world – few often get to enjoy a behind-the-scenes peek at just how much effort and planning goes into game development or book research or even orchestrating a public event. For your backers, this can provide an extra reward, and one that keeps your project fresh in their minds and may even attract new fans.

As a general rule though, once campaigns have concluded, your community should be migrated over to dedicated websites, blogs, or other persistent online solutions where your project will live on in perpetuity. Not only will such destinations serve as a stable, reliable and centralized home for all news and updates related to your project, with no fear of eventual page removal or deletion. They'll also allow you to push topical announcements to the forefront, and make a much better tool for maintaining long-term conversations with fans than crowdfunding sites themselves.

How you stay connected will depend on the type of project you are working on, your personal style and how much effort you can expend on outreach. In the end, it can be a highly rewarding experience, and could even lead to some great insights and suggestions from your fans.

# CONTRIBUTING TO YOUR COMMUNITY

**"Some people think crowdfunding is simply about an investment. It's not. They think it's easy, free money even… It isn't. There's no such thing. Crowdfunding [and connecting with fans] is a big obligation, and you need to correspond with them constantly and keep things moving."**

- Jordan Weisman, *Shadowrun Returns*

## Pay Your Taxes

Also, be aware of the potential tax implications of any investment dollars raised via crowdfunding campaigns. Consult a certified professional, such as your financial advisor or CPA, regarding how and when taxes must be paid on this income, and allocate funds appropriately. Note that initial research to this extent should always take place before you launch your campaign. You will want to pay close attention to when your campaign ends relative to the end of each tax year, and how any unspent portion of income generated thereby will be treated at the end of that period.

# High Score 3: A Kickstarter Postmortem

The situation: I needed to create a new edition of my popular video games industry history book, *High Score*, which was currently out of print. The dilemma: I was out of work, meaning that I had time, but no obvious source of income. The solution: Kickstarter – or so it would seem. Ever wonder what goes into running a crowdfunding campaign? Allow me to take you behind the scenes…

## Part 1: Getting Started

When I first started my Kickstarter project – a sequel to mine and Johnny Wilson's popular video games industry history book – I was acutely aware of the recent success of Tim Schafer, whose development studio Double Fine asked for $400,000 and ended up making more than $3.3 million. If he could make that much, I reasoned, I could achieve a lesser goal without much trouble. After all, I had a good project, was promoting the sequel to a bestselling book, enjoyed many connections with prominent industry insiders, and boasted the support of lots of friends. Everything should go smoothly, right?

So I did some research, looked at projects that were working and read all the material that Kickstarter's staff offers to help project creators prepare. I worked for a week on my video pitch and initial presentation of the project, my rewards for backers and a number of other minute details, such as the total funding amount I would ask for and the overall project timeline. I thought I had it all figured out and was, finally and with some trepidation, ready to launch. In retrospect, pushing that button was like launching myself into empty space without a parachute. I was committed. I was excited. I was terrified. Little did I know where we would eventually land.

The risk we all take when we turn to solutions like Kickstarter is that people won't respond – our perfectly valid fear being that we'll fail and look foolish. Our egos are involved. Are we going to be picked for the football team, or the one that everybody ignores? And ultimately, just what do we have to do to be successful?

I knew from the start that involving social media as an element of the campaign would be critical, and that I would have to market the project relentlessly. I had my main networks all lined up and ready to go – Facebook, Twitter and LinkedIn, specifically. But I'm not a social media powerhouse – hell, I'm barely a rusty, old fusebox by modern standards. I have friends, but I rarely post updates. I usually can't think of anything to say that I think other people will find interesting.

I also knew that rewards would be important, and that the most natural reward to offer fans would be a copy of the book, or an autographed edition. But I faced the problem that the books themselves and shipping would be costly, however, and funds for all would eventually come out of my own pocket – so at first I limited the number of book rewards being offered. Ultimately, I felt, my aces in the hole were the meals with famous designers I could offer everyday fans – letting them enjoy the once-in-a-lifetime chance to savor the company of such legendary game makers as Will Wright, Trip Hawkins, Lorne Lanning, John Romero, Peter Molyneux, Sid Meier and more. About 20 industry legends in all volunteered to contribute, each of whom had generously offered of their time. Looking back, I'm certain that it is because of their support that I was eventually successful.

## Part 2: Backer Support

Day one was good. *High Score 3* gained interest from quite a few backers right away, and things were looking promising. But by day two, I quickly realized to my chagrin that this was going to be a long haul, and that I had a lot of work to do. Translation: The project's momentum had slowed down – and by a considerable factor.

Over the first week, I kept spreading the word amongst fans and journalists, and in fact blasted a media advisory out to a huge list of press outlets that I had gathered. Over the subsequent weeks, I did several interviews and even wrote a couple of articles as promotional pieces. However, what helped me immensely in those early days, more so than any actual stories written, was the feedback from my backers. I heard from people who were major fans of the book, who provided a tremendous confidence boost and extra motivation, and many of them offered me help in improving the project.

Interestingly, the first thing fans noted was that I had to give away more books – so I bit the bullet and offered unlimited book rewards, setting prices at $50 for the book itself and $70 for an autographed copy. Unsurprisingly (hint: listening to your audience can't be undervalued) this helped. It turns out that people like books – as a veteran author, you'd think I might have noticed. I also added additional rewards, such as rewarding every person who donated $10 or more by putting their name in the book, and awarding special mentions to those who donated $1000 or $2500.

The project cheerfully began to pick up steam again, and was moving forward to the tune of about $1000 per day. I still wasn't sure if it was going to succeed, but I kept adding rewards and updating the project, listening to my backers and accepting all the help I could get. One exceptionally devoted fan even offered to produce a limited edition comic book as a low-cost reward, and many people were interested in that. I also added a t-shirt option, which people liked.

Nonetheless, there were still very slow days throughout the campaign when my doubts resurfaced. I watched my friend Brian Fargo make $500,000 in 17 hours with his admittedly very cool project to reboot classic role-playing game Wasteland with a sequel decades after its initial debut. But as happy for him as I was, I had to admit: While all this was going on, I was still struggling to get to $25K. I kept asking myself: Had I done something wrong? Why weren't people flocking to my project?

But the good news is that I eventually came to realize that each project has its own resonance, its own lifecycle and its own audience. Books on gaming history don't compare sales-wise with amazing video games by great designers. I got over my frustration and moved on

– and as my mood picked up, so did my enthusiasm and creativity, and fans responded in kind. My project continued to move slowly, but steadily toward its goal.

## Part 3: Setbacks

As is so often the case, just when things were looking up, and the project was beginning to advance, we began to hit a couple of snags. First, game publisher Taito wouldn't let me use a Space Invader image on my promotional T-shirt, so I had to scramble to create a new design. That wasn't so bad – more a personal disappointment than anything major.

But what really shook me was discovering that my publisher was going to set the retail price of the book at $50 and was going to give me a far smaller discount on the books than I had initially anticipated. So, once I computed my costs, it became apparent that for every $50 book I was offering, about $30 of it went to cover raw expenses. This immediately changed the nature of the project, and its supporting budget, and was an example of me not doing all my homework before setting prices and launching the project – a classic entrepreneurial error. I was caught by surprise, but shouldn't have been. As such, it's a lesson I want to share with other aspiring startups and creators: Be sure you've factored in all your costs up-front, and budgeted in some wiggle room in case of unforeseen events, so you don't get blindsided in mid-stream like I did.

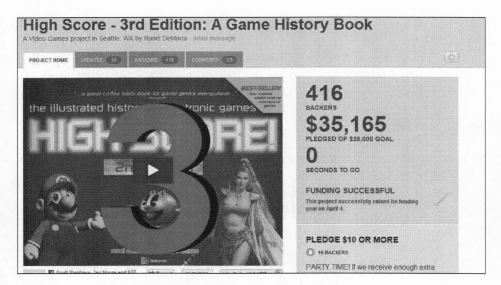

Also worth noting: I posted an update about these issues, which resulted in many people blaming the publisher and putting a negative spin on things. Let me be clear: I don't blame the publisher – they've been very kind and supportive, in fact. The print business is difficult, and

I know that they are doing all they can to support the *High Score 3* project. But I was still distressed at that time.

Then I got a message from an industry friend – the kind of friend who tells you the cold, hard truth, and she told me that the negativity, and depressing news, was a turnoff. And, quite wisely, pointed out that I needed to keep things on a positive note and to encourage people to believe in the project, reminding me that audiences often pick up on these cues – and that dissent spreads faster than optimism. She was right, and I realized that I still had a lot to learn about marketing a product or managing an event. It was a humbling lesson, and one gratefully accepted.

And in the end, I ultimately worked things out with the publisher, who wound up donating a number of books to the project – enough so that it took much of the pain away. Lesson learned: Positivity and professionalism are crucial to the success of any campaign, and it never pays to burn bridges. Happily, as the project entered its final week, two sources stepped up and gave me $2500 in angel donations. These contributions ultimately turned the tide of the project and made it possible for us to meet and exceed our initial goal.

## Part 4: Completion

I have to say that High Score 3's life as a Kickstarter project was both exhilarating and an emotional rollercoaster at the same time. At one point, during an especially low period, I really thought I was going to fail, and that brought up a lot of distress and personal issues. But there were great times, too, when I would hear from fans of my book, telling me how much they have enjoyed the volume over the years, and, in some cases, how High Score actually changed their lives for the better.

In the end, I'm tremendously grateful that I took the risk and pressed that Launch button. Of course, I'm also glad that I found a safe landing spot, and am now able to move forward on the 3rd edition of the book. For all the good times and bad, I suppose it's worth noting: If I had to do it over again, I would – only I'd be better prepared. Ultimately, I'm extremely grateful to all of the people who backed the project, and those who made tremendous contributions in terms of their time, support and advice. Thank you all, and thank you twice over for giving me the opportunity to share these experiences. I sincerely hope the lessons learned will aid you in your future ventures – you've certainly helped us in the making of High Score, and me to personally grow and learn from the experience.

**- Rusel DeMaria**

# Conclusion

Having read this manuscript, it should by now be patently obvious: While crowdfunding is one of the most exciting things to happen to entrepreneurs and startups in decades, and offers considerable upsides, it isn't for everyone. However, it may provide just the spark of ignition your company needs to take off – and rocket into the stratosphere. Yes, great risks exist, just as they do with any other method of raising capital or attracting investors. But rewards far outweigh potential drawbacks for many of today's most savvy creators, including both experienced entrepreneurs and everyday individuals alike.

Moreover, for the independent creator, crowdfunding presents one of the most exciting means of raising project capital seen in decades, and most promising ways to gauge consumer appetite for new ideas witnessed in the history of the industry. Similar to the shareware revolution of the 1990s which made companies like id Software and games like DOOM multi-million dollar franchises and household names, its potential seems boundless. Not only does the phenomenon potentially allow entrepreneurs and startups with great ideas to directly connect with, attract, and tap into the support of a new or existing fan base. It also allows creators with wildly new and original ideas, or those who've been previously rebuffed by unsympathetic investors, to greatly mitigate the risks presented with new ventures by making it possible to do so prior to product completion.

Worth noting: Crowdfunding and pre-retailing will inevitably change how some types of projects are financed at a fundamental level. Just as services like Amazon.com and eBay have transformed how new products are marketed and sold, and used products recycled and monetized, consider: Crowdfunding sites such as Kickstarter, its peers and successors could very well revolutionize how products are conceived, tested, retailed and marketed; consumers interact with their favorite brands; and the way in which surrounding communities of like-minded individuals are developed, nurtured and maintained.

But don't get too swept away in the hype. An entirely new form of investing and retailing, crowdfunding is also experiencing considerable growing pains as it fights to gain legitimacy, comply with international law, and attract a burgeoning audience of supporters, composed of both financial backers and inventors alike. Destined to be subject to significant swings in consumer expectation, competition, and demand, tomorrow's crowdfunding industry may look little like what we see today. As such, staying up to date on current trends and market forces influencing the business is critical. The shape of project pitches, and the sites that host and facilitate them, will greatly change over time.

Also important to bear in mind: Crowdfunding is a marathon, not a sprint. As with any startup venture, succeeding with the methodology requires extensive planning and forethought – and the skill and flexibility to change and adapt to new developments on a dime. To achieve success in crowdfunded ventures, you not only need to understand your target audience; how to reach and speak to them; and be able to communicate your vision clearly, as well as construct a compelling argument for your product. You must also be able to assemble, mobilize and empower a community of partners, fans, friends and supporters, and sustain their awareness in what is at heart a fickle and ever-changing industry.

Moreover, it pays to remember: Even when campaigns end, the work doesn't – you can't afford to forget about backers once fundraising campaigns have concluded. As your most ardent brand evangelists, best customers, and those certain to be first in line the next time your new project idea hits, it's vital to give them the attention and respect that they deserve. Think hard about how to engage with them and keep conversations running – they're the essential glue that holds crowdfunding together, and are helping propel the practice's future to new and previously unforeseen heights.

The good news for both inventors and innovators is that crowdfunding is becoming more publicly recognized and legitimized as a means of funding projects with each passing day. Better still, given the continued popularity of new programs like Kicking it Forward and growing number of solutions rapidly becoming available to self-starters, the sky's the limit. (VentureBeat actually estimates that Kickstarter could raise $300 million in 2012 alone – three times as much as the year prior.) Whether going it solo, or turning to other experienced creators to help fund new crowdfunding ventures, opportunities bring great ideas to life – and be successful doing so – suddenly abound. True, the field will only become more competitive. But if you're prepared, and truly have something to offer audiences for the better, it's worth the effort. In the end, you have preciously little to lose by attempting to crowdfund a venture, and the fulfillment of your dreams to gain.

Ready to get started? We sincerely hope that you've found this guide to be of service. Now fasten your seatbelt and get ready to go to work. As should be patently obvious, there's a long, winding and potentially wonderful road that lies ahead – not to mention one that promises to be exhilarating and exhausting in equal measure. Good luck in your crowdfunding ventures!

---

## BE DIFFERENT

**"Be creative, go crazy, make up some wacky new perks or do something totally different [with your campaign]. The whole crowdfunding initiative is fresh – so don't be boring. Take chances, as only positive things that can come from them. We live in an amazing age where a couple of people in a basement can create a feature film and distribute it worldwide. Don't take that for granted."**

- Brad Crawford, *100 Yen: The Japanese Arcade Experience*

---

# Expert Hints and Tips

## Scott Wilson – Founder of Design Studio MINIMAL

One of the early adopters of the crowdfunding model, Scott's innovative design for a watchband and holder for Apple's iPod Nano (including the TikTok and LunaTik Multi-Touch watch kits) resulted in one of the first smash successes on Kickstarter, grossing nearly $1 million in just 30 days. We talked with Scott about what it was like to be on the bleeding edge of this new form of investment.

**Q.** You used Kickstarter before most people even knew what it was. What led you there?

**A:** Rejection. I'd been working for a while on a design for a more premium watchband for the Nano (I didn't want it to be just another rubber strap, but something that complemented Apple's design). I showed it around to a few people, a number of companies, and they would all have initial interest, and then they'd pass. One of my friends, a former designer, had left and gone to work on Obama's campaign as design director, and he ran a campaign on Kickstarter called Designing Obama, that had done pretty well. So that was the point I first noticed crowdfunding.

Around the time I was getting all these rejections, I also noticed that the Glif [iPhone 4 tripod mount] guys and the success they were having and I thought, "Well, why don't I put this up there and see what happens? Otherwise this design is just going to sit in a folder on my computer and die."

At that time, there weren't that many products like mine to look at, so I looked at what had been done with *Designing Obama* and how its creator did a nice little video, as well as what others were doing, and everything seemed pretty raw, approachable and real. A lot of what we do for or design clients, well, my thinking was if I could do at least half as good as that, then that would be fine for the Kickstarter platform.

I had some rendering and the prototypes that we built, and from that we put together a video, and I would talk about my background, which I hoped would lend some credibility. Then we added an animation showing how it would fit together and some b-roll stuff from 'behind the scenes' making the product. I remember that it was a couple of week's worth of work, and the guys in the office were busy and would occasionally ask, "Why are you wasting your time on all that?"

**Q.** Public relations and marketing: How did you handle them?

**A:** Pre-launch, I really only had one conversation with *Fast Company* in New York. Before I had even thought of Kickstarter, I'd shown them images on my phone of what I wanted to do and they fell in love with it and wanted to break the story of what we were doing. So that's how things began.

And then coincidentally, the day before we launched the campaign, I had just hired a PR agency for the Minimal, and when she started I stepped her through all the stuff that needed doing; here's the stuff for MINIMAL, stuff for design awards, and a bunch of other things that I don't like to deal with, and oh, by the way there's this Kickstarter thing tomorrow, and there may be a little bit of stuff to do there. And when it hit, it just went crazy, and she was fielding all the inquiries and also reaching out to the major blogs. She dealt with all that stuff and filtered it for me – that turned out to be great timing.

We had a pretty good idea of who we thought would be interested in TikTok: Apple geeks, watch collectors and folks like that… but what we didn't know was how many. We underestimated how many we could reach when we connected the dots of storytelling, PR and social media, and what would happen when a viral loop established itself.

We really had no idea how well it would sell; our budget was based on covering the tooling, and a minimum order quantity that we'd have to commit to with our overseas manufacturer of maybe 5000 pieces over the course of a year. My biggest concern with the whole campaign was that we'd post it up there, but how would anybody find out about it? So I put it up the night before, maybe around midnight, and I watched it, and in the morning only one person had pledged.

*Fast Company* ran the exclusive the morning of the launch, and that was maybe 8:30am. Then it got a little momentum and by 5:30pm that day we were at about $6,000 and we left the office all excited because we were halfway there. I was heading to a bar to meet up with a friend, and on the way I get a text message from my wife that it was at $22,000, and I thought, "She must be looking at the wrong project." A few minutes later I get another text that it's at $30,000, and I thought, "What the hell?" We found out later that this was when the piece on TikTok went live on *Gizmodo*.

And then the email on my phone starts going nuts. "Ding, Ding, Ding da Ding." By the end of that night, we were at close to $100,000. That was our first big spike, and then they ran a second, follow-up piece a couple of weeks later, and that was our second biggest spike. And then after something like that, people start sharing the story, social media comes into play, and it starts to feed on itself.

I'd like to say we planned it: The time of year we picked to do it, the tech blogs we reached out to, a sort of "What if we did these things, what would happen?" – but it really did take on a life of its own. The project turned out to have a much wider appeal than we thought. Different people saw different things in it, and it resonated for them. It's a thing that's hard to repeat, but then you see what's happening with the Pebble Watch, and Double Fine's adventure and how people get caught up in it… and it's cool.

So definitely find out who the influencers are for your type of product. Especially on social networks: Who is that one person who is going to be the tipping point for you?

# Q. Managing the campaign and the after-campaign process: Mind sharing how it went?

**A:** Ugh! It was a lot of work to manage. You definitely don't want to underestimate maintenance and follow-up. I was pretty much dedicated from the campaign launch until the spring when we hired some folks to take it over. We actually hired some people to help me make sure that we didn't lose any messages through the cracks as people would message and email me. I think at one point we had a total of maybe 40,000 messages to deal with and it was overwhelming. I was constantly responding to these messages and questions. It was fun, but took quite a bit of time. You're probably going to want to recruit some help for this part.

Interestingly, one of the decisions that we made in the final week was to quickly put up a pre-order site at the end to capture some of the momentum after the campaign ended. We probably got another $70,000 preorders the day after the campaign ended, putting us over $1 million in total pledges. And that momentum really didn't slow down much in the next couple of weeks.

Another thing that we did that was shockingly successful was to ask everybody over on our Kickstarter page to go over to our product website and sign up for the newsletter. We probably got a conversion rate of nearly 10% in just the first eight hours. It just showed how much enthusiasm the early adopters had to hear more about the project as things went on.

# Q. Anything you'd do differently if you had to do it all again?

**A:** One of the biggest worries I had when TikTok went big was how to fulfill it globally. I was traveling in China while the Kickstarter campaign was going on and happened to post an update (shot with my iPhone and complied with iMovie – again, on my phone) and one of the biggest fulfillment guys in all of Asia saw the update (he must have been monitoring the project) and got a hold of me, "Hey, I see you're in China, I'm sending a car to pick you up. I want to fulfill your product globally for you." That was a HUGE relief off of my shoulders when that happened.

Don't underestimate the execution side of things. I'll occasionally get emails from folks who'll say sometime like, "I successfully funded my project, but now I don't know what to do!" Do your homework. On the bright side, when all was said and done, we shipped out 22,000 units to over 50 countries.

# Q. What sort of impact did the crowdfunding campaign have for your company and project?

**A:** The thing I get everywhere I go, and the thing I find most rewarding when I talk to folks who've started their own campaigns, is "You were my inspiration to do it myself." That will last long after the TikTok and the Lunatik are gone; when Apple has moved on and the

Nano's design is different, that source of inspiration will still be there. Obviously, Kickstarter built the platform, but I think we helped a little bit to build awareness and showed product designers that "hey, there's something here." It probably would have happened eventually – we just happened to be in the right place with the right product.

## Stephen Toulouse – Author and Former Director of Policy for Microsoft's Xbox Live

Stephen campaigned on Kickstarter.com for his latest book, *After: A Series of Stories Following the Events of Feb. 22nd*. We spoke with him about Kickstarter and how it changed his outlook on publishing.

### Q. Why turn to crowdfunding as a source of raising investment?

A: I had just left my job at Microsoft's Xbox division after 18 years with the company. My intent was to try and make writing a full-time profession, and I had two projects nearing completion. Both of them are nonfiction projects and were entering the "tedious" phase where working on them wasn't as much fun as a third project I had been contemplating. That third project is a fiction project and is the one I chose to fund using Kickstarter. Under the traditional publishing model, a writer submits ideas to a publisher and if the writer is well-known or the idea is good enough, then the publisher might allow for an advance against royalties for the writer. The writer then uses those funds to live off of while the project is completed. I'd had several friends successfully fund projects using Kickstarter and that seemed like a great way to handle the project instead. The only concern I had about crowdfunding was not making the goal! Since I set it fairly low (just the amount I needed to self publish, pay for my editor, etc.) it would have probably been a vote of no confidence in the project!

### Q. How did you go about putting together the campaign?

A: The only research I did was through Kickstarter's own education system once you set up your account. They do a great job of telling you what projects tend to be successfully funded, what mistakes to avoid, and your responsibilities as a creator. I have a fairly close relationship to my fan base from my previous book, A Microsoft Life, so I decided that while I was going to crowdfund, I wasn't going to actually go the route of wanting to pick up a ton of money that way. Then I ran my idea for the project itself by many people to gauge interest and to hone the "pitch." This step is, I think, critical. There are a lot of crowdfunding options out there now, and a lot of projects being crowdfunded: You have to make sure your idea is easily explained and that your pitch really cuts to why someone would want to be a part of making it happen.

## Q. What type of content did you assemble for it, and how did you put it together?

**A:** As mentioned above, a concise and compelling project description is key. The world of crowdfunding isn't as cutthroat as, say, the world of venture capitalism... but that doesn't change the fact that the more thought-out your description, the likelier people are to believe it's going to be a real thing. The second thing that's critical is to provide either previous work or established work that people can go look at to determine value. If it's your first project or product, consider providing samples or other items that people can read or look over to see you've actually put some thought into this and the idea that they are funding isn't just some daydream.

I decided to go simple and create everything myself. I find you don't have to overdo it, as most of the successful funded projects I have seen concentrate on communicating a lot about the project to the funder and not going the route of flashy hand waving. My advice is to make sure you're getting across what you are making, why you want to make it, and what you plan to use the money for to bring the project to life.

## Q. Any advice for designing more effective campaign rewards?

**A:** With respect to rewards, make them collaborative! The difference between someone who won't try out an app for .99 cents, but will happily pitch in $5 to a Kickstarter campaign seems to be the latter person's feeling of involvement in the project. For mine, I defined several levels of rewards that involve contributors receiving the finished work, but alongside that I also put in customized notes of thanks, special limited versions just for Kickstarter funders, and at one tier I even offered to write the funder into the work as a character! The second piece of advice I'd offer here is to have many levels of rewards and have at least one reward be at a low entry point, e.g. $5. This allows your backers to choose their level of involvement easily and having a low entry tier will more often than not result in a funded project!

## Q. How about funding goals – what tips would you offer there?

**A:** In my case, I think setting the funding request amount was probably the most critical thing I focused on. I thought long and hard about what the amount should be, and why I was actually doing all this in the first place. I had two projects near completion that would earn money, and this third project that I really wanted to do, but couldn't really justify given that I wasn't working at the time. So I set the amount at just the amount I would need to actually publish the work. Based on my previous experience for a book this size, I arrived at a funding goal of roughly $1,000. Again, I wasn't trying to earn a level of book advance that I would be able to live off of… rather, I was looking for a funding justification to shift my attention to this project over the others. It's very tempting to ask for too much, or even too little! I would say once you come up with a figure you want to ask for, spend a lot of time really attacking that number. What assumptions are you making in arriving at it? What if something unexpected happens? What if your costs are variable as opposed to fixed? Most importantly, if it gets funded, but that amount turns out to not quite be enough, what reserves do you have that you yourself can put into play beyond the funding that will help ensure you can get the project out the door?

## Q. How did you go about putting together your marketing and media campaign?

**A:** I did it myself by leveraging my Twitter followers, Facebook friends, a series of podcasts, and my personal blog. I would guess that the vast majority of my funders were already fans when I put the Kickstarter campaign up. I recommend selling people on your idea at your crowdfunding site, then using social media to point people there. Too often I see people throw their message out equally on blogs, podcasts, and other platforms. All I did was continually remind my followers and fans that I had a Kickstarter page, and to please visit it for more information. The more you move the meat of communicating your idea to different places, the more you dilute the one call to action you need to remind them of most: Getting people to click on the button that lets them donate. I might read your entire pitch on your blog and agree [with the sentiment], but might miss the fact that I have to go to one other place to actually help you. If your crowdfunding site allows for embedding buttons or other methods of attracting attention, that's OK. Just remember that you want to be selling your idea at the closest possible distance from the backer's ability to help you.

## Q. Some of the best ways creators can promote their projects include...?

**A:** Striking the balance between social media promotion and spamming your followers is a tough act. But I found that continually mentioning the Kickstarter campaign on my Twitter feed every other day or so seemed to always spur interest and donations. The lowest pricing tier, set at $5, was one of the most popular tiers and ended up accounting for over a third of the original funding request amount. Interest in the higher-level tiers naturally slowed down, but I also chose to provide limited tiers where only so many funders could give at that amount, and limit them due to the personalized nature of the reward I was giving them. These sold out in minutes!

Twitter was enormously helpful [as a promotional tool] too. Facebook, not so much. I think that's mostly because Facebook is a complex experience, meaning people are there to post photos and read status updates and play games. It's easy for a blurb about a project to get missed while you play FarmVille. Twitter users, however, seem particularly engaged with their streams, and there's nothing else really to distract them.

# Q. How did things go after you launched?

**A:** One mistake I made was that I waited to engage backers until the project was fund-ed. Then I sent out an update asking what people liked in terms of engagement. I didn't want to spam people, but also wanted them to know that I was engaged and using the money for what I said I would use it for. Every couple of weeks I send a big update to the list with samples of work, etc. Unlike other campaigns, once I set the rewards, I also chose not to change anything. I worked probably a dozen hours (before the campaign launched) on defining the rewards and thinking about them. I think if you do a good job of nailing your reward tiers that you typically don't have to adjust them later.

# Q. Any parting thoughts?

**A:** My Kickstarter campaign was overfunded by 630%, so it's tempting to say that I should have asked for more money. But the reality is it overfunded precisely because I was clear about what I was going to do with the funds, and I truly asked for what I needed as opposed to hoping or planning on getting more. Probably the biggest stumbling block was not realizing how long it takes to setup a campaign on the site. Kickstarter wants to verify your identity as well as review and approve the actual project. It wasn't a huge delay, taking roughly around four days, but I wasn't prepared for it and had to change my launch date to accommodate my travel schedule.

On the bright side, crowdfunding returns the relationship between artists/creators and their customers to one of direct patronage instead of the current model which requires some mono-lithic entity like a publisher to stand in the way. My biggest piece of advice here to anyone run-ning a campaign is to engage with your backers! People want to be a part of awesome things, and for a lot of people the only way they can do that is through donation or participating in crowdfunding. Tell people precisely what you are creating, and once they fund you, don't end that relationship! Keep them close and updated and you will find that they will be that much more willing to support you again.

# Ed Petterson – Musician, Writer and Producer

Ed's musical credits are far too numerous to list here, but he's probably best known as the co-producer of the acclaimed compilation *Song of America*. Recently, he launched a campaign to produce and distribute a recording by Giuseppi Logan, hailed as one of the bright lights of free jazz, and a contemporary of John Coltrane. In the '70s, Giuseppi disappeared from view and remained lost to the music world for over 30 years, until 2009, when he was found playing for change in New York. Truly a labor of love, Ed saw an opportunity to bring Guiseppi's work to contemporary fans of jazz music with his campaign, and, as he puts it, "support a legendary jazz player in his love of making music."

## Q. What turned you on to crowdfunding?

**A:** I had approached several record labels for the project, but all of them turned us down. Almost all in fact, without even hearing the work we'd created. Frankly, this pissed me off, but it isn't uncommon given the state of the record industry. Undaunted and somewhat emboldened by the rejections, I decided to take matters into my own hands (I've done this pretty much my whole music career). I had heard about Kickstarter for a couple of years and have some friends who've used it successfully, so I thought I'd give it a shot.

Actually, I wasn't a big fan of crowdfunding. To me, it had a tinge of begging and the recording industry is humiliating enough without adding to it. However, when it was pointed out to me that in essence we were simply pre-selling our wares to fans we already had and potentially new ones as well, I realized that my prejudice was silly.

I thought that the reclamation of a heralded jazz legend was a compelling tale. Giuseppi had been missing for almost 40 years after a highly respected start in the '60s. The fact that he was homeless, penniless and so in love with music that he was playing for change in a New York City park made me believe that other people may be as moved as I was.

## Q. How did you plot and assemble your campaign?

**A:** I did copious research. We studied several, maybe even dozens of campaigns… why some were working, why others weren't, why some were more attractive than others, etc. We also looked at which promotional devices they were using, what their networks were, and so forth. We actually spent about a week or ten days studying other campaigns.

We used some of the more effective campaigns we studied as a jumping off point, but then followed the Kickstarter tutorial to the letter. We made a video, wrote a deep and compelling story, and explained the project as completely as possible: Kickstarter actually has copy on their site about this. Then we spent about four to five days writing and rewriting, all the while referring back to some of the more successful campaigns we saw.

My advice here: Study as many campaigns as possible! Take time to do the research. And take your time: I truly believe that a successful campaign is very carefully considered and composed. But even then, there are no guarantees. If it wasn't for a stroke of luck, getting a prime The New York Times cover story, we may not have reached our goal (although we in fact far surpassed it). We spent four hours a day for three weeks after our campaign launched writing to every jazz journalist, every blog, every website and every record collector we could find. We sent out hundreds of individual e-mails and letters. We did our homework and worked hard…. but ultimately got lucky.

# Q. How did launching and marketing the campaign go?

A: We didn't have any money left after creating the work (the recorded music album) after we had finished. So the launching, PR and marketing was all on my wife and I. (She's actually the real brains of the operation!) No doubt, though, The New York Times article was the most successful coverage we received. Before it, after three weeks of extremely hard work, we had raised $855. After it, we'd raised $11,550.

One thing I will say is that print is not dead: Blogs are great, but overrated frankly. We spent so much effort and got little tangible return until that effort attracted a large, respected newspaper's attention. It's hard to say what was the least effective [strategy we used], because somehow all roads led to getting The New York Times interested in our project. They obviously heard about it from someone we had contacted, i.e. a blog, activist, or other journalist.

When it comes to marketing your campaign, be very careful about being honest with yourself about the true reach and breadth of your project and its potential. Ask friends and foes for feedback before you spend the time and effort. Sometimes it's good to hear the bad and good before you gauge whether it's worth it to dive in.

That said, after the campaign launched, I personally thanked each and every person who pledged, immediately after they pledged. This, I think, is very important. Some folks haven't been exposed to crowdfunding before, and providing personal info and contacts. I believe it's prudent, polite and comforting for them to hear from us right away. It seals the deal, if you will. We also have posted two general updates to the entire group of funders to keep them connected and involved. After the campaign, we plan to write to them at least once a week and actually deliver the final product long before anticipated. We also plan on offering bonus perks before finally delivering like other music we've recorded from other projects for free.

# Q. What does Guiseppi think of all of this? And how do you think this will impact the development of projects like this or even something like Song of America?

A: I don't quite know what he thinks. I know he's overwhelmed by the goodwill and generosity of the people who have come to his aid, and he's rejuvenated by it and maybe a little validated. But since he's been around a while, you might say he thinks it's pretty wild!

I wish we had this when we did Song of America. The Song of America project was very successful by almost anyone's standards and won many awards, but it may have reached even more people than it did [had we done it through crowdfunding], and given us the resources to do more. For example: We had originally intended to provide each public school in America with a teaching guide to go with the music album, and in fact professor Dean Roote of the University of Pittsburgh has created it, but we fell short of funding to realize this goal.

# Q. What lasting lessons would you say you learned from the effort?

**A:** The biggest stumbling block that we encountered was the immense number of social media outlets, blogs and websites that you need to reach, and even then there are no guarantees. Also, a lot of these people are insulted if you send them mass cc e-mails. Obviously, writing to each one individually is a large commitment.

[If I had to do it again], I also would have tried to meet with as many people in the jazz community in person as possible before we started. Yes, it would have been time-consuming and maybe somewhat not feasible financially and physically, but it could have made a difference.

Also worth keeping in mind: Once you do decide to dive in, you must be relentless. Nothing will come easy, and it may take up a good deal of your time, but once you commit, work harder than you ever imagined or you will regret it and may lose the opportunity. Campaigns won't be easy, but can be very rewarding… and exhausting, for that matter.

## Jake Parker – Artist and Illustrator

Jake Parker is the creator of the graphic novel series *Missile Mouse* from Scholastic, illustrator of *The New York Times* bestselling picture book *Awesome Man,* and has developed concept art for animated features such as *Horton Hears a Who, Ice Age III,* and *Rio.* When Jake decided that he wanted to publish a collection of all of the short comic stories he'd been drawing over the past eight years, he turned to crowdfunding.

## Q. Why use online fundraising techniques to bring in investment dollars for your project?

**A:** My book has such a niche market that both my agent and I felt that it wouldn't be of interest to publishers. I've self-published before, and it's hard to get exposure. Kickstarter seemed the perfect platform to launch this project from.

I had been watching Kickstarter for a year or so. I watched both the most successful campaigns and those that didn't reach their funding goals. I took note of what worked and what didn't. The big takeaway from watching these projects unfold was as follows: Presentation is key. I knew for my project to be successful that it had to look expertly done and presented in a clean and professional way.

Going into this, I had a good idea of who my target audience was. I met with a group of them to see if there was interest in something like my book. The response was overwhelmingly positive, so I proceeded with the project.

**Q.** **Where else did you turn for support and advice when plotting your campaign?**

**A:** A big help was being able to talk directly to others who had conducted successful Kickstarter campaigns. If I didn't know them, I introduced myself in an email and set up a time to Skype with them. In every instance, they were extremely open and helpful. I also shared my project plans with friends and family who were from different demographics so that I could get their unique perspectives. Feedback ranged from commentary from retirees in their sixties to input from twenty-somethings still in college to contemporaries in my field. Some suggested offering lower pricing and pledge levels, while others thought I should raise the costs associated with each pricing tier. Some said I didn't have enough information in my pitch, and others said that I was too specific. So I took all of these thoughts and decided which were best for this project.

**Q.** **What steps were involved in the actual production of the campaign?**

**A:** The main thing I wanted done well, and knew that I wouldn't be able to do on my own, was the video. I always watch the videos which appear on Kickstarter, and I've seen everything from webcam recordings to professionally-done clips. So to produce mine, I called in a favor from a guy I work with who does video. We made a deal that we'd exchange services. He'd put together a little video for me, and I'd draw up something nice for a project he was doing.

The rest involved coming up with a cohesive visual style that presented the material and read well. I used [software program] Adobe Photoshop to put all my images together.

**Q.** **How did you go about designing your rewards?**

**A:** My approach was to make something for everyone. There are people out there with just a little cash on-hand, and then there are the guys who just got a bonus and are looking to burn it – I wanted make something for all. But the bread and butter of your funding will come from offering a reasonable reward for a reasonable amount of money to reasonable people. So make sure there's something for them too. Otherwise, I contacted printers and got quotes for how much my books would cost. I calculated shipping costs, and factored in the amount that Kickstarter and Amazon take from contributions, and I factored in a little extra for unexpected hiccups as well.

**Q.** **How did you handle the launch, PR and marketing campaign?**

**A:** I'm small-time so I did it all myself. My strategy came about by looking at what had worked for others and seeing if any of these strategies applied to me, determining what options did and then implementing them. My advice is to already have a strong relationship with your audience before you ask for money. People can smell a rat. As for my top tip: Use Twitter and Kickstarter. Twitter spread the word so fast and got people excited. That drove up the popularity of my project and got it on the popular page at Kickstarter, which drove many more eyes to my page.

## Q. What about the post-launch phase – how's that working out?

A: It's so much more time-consuming than I had expected. The main interaction with my community happens at Twitter, so it's no different than during the campaign. People ask me questions there, and I answer them there. But I do suggest making time to build your community before launching the campaign. Make them fans first, then they'll back whatever you do.

# Brad Crawford – Writer/Director of 100 Yen: The Japanese Arcade Experience

Following in the footsteps blazed by breakout Kickstarter film success *Indie Game: The Movie*, the idea for Brad Crawford's motion picture *100 Yen* first began to germinate when he visited Japan for a wedding. Armed with a camera, Brad spent the spare time before and after the celebration capturing scenes from Japan's iconic arcades, which have flourished throughout the nation, despite their boom then meteoric decline in the West. From these initial efforts emerged a trailer and the reel used for Crawford's IndieGoGo campaign, which gave a documentary film which otherwise might never have seen the light of day a chance at being screened for the general public.

## Q. How did things first come together for the project?

A: *100 Yen* began with a journey to Japan on my own dime. I was visiting the country for a friend's wedding and thought it made sense to spend the time productively and capture a piece of its culture. From there, I ended up with a trailer that I thought represented an idea for a film.

For me, having something [visual to show like this] is a key step towards launching a crowdfunding campaign. It also helped that some local filmmakers (namely, Blinkworks of *Indie Game: The Movie* fame) had just raised $20,000 via Kickstarter, and I was able to wrack their brains for tips and advice.

I had very little concern regarding attempting to use crowdfunding, actually. I approached it as if it was this attractive female that I had always had a crush on and suddenly got the guts to ask out. If she said no, nothing would change. But if she said yes? Just imagine. The benefits of a campaign outweigh any negative aspects that could arise, at least from my perspective. The fact that both campaigns we've run have been successful might skew my opinion slightly, however.

The main reason I thought the campaign would work was 1. I had just witnessed *Indie Game: The Movie*'s massive success with a similar concept and 2. I felt like [fans with an interest in] video games and Japan were two very large demographics that should be fairly easy to locate and advertise to online.

As mentioned, I spoke with the creators of *Indie Game: The Movie* and studied their campaign, and essentially used their method as a jumping off point for my own campaigns. My target demographic was fairly clear-cut and it helped that I frequent a number of the major sites that are involved with both gaming and Japanese lifestyle. Another key part of the entire campaign was having [notable personalities on our side] like Brian Ashcraft who helped push the film via Kotaku and Ryan Gutierrez who is a well-known figure within the fighting game scene. Both of these figures helped lend credibility to the project and promote it through different media outlets.

As the product I'm creating is a film, I poured all of my energy into creating the best product I could. If I could intrigue viewers with the video, then they would be willing to support my ideas and trust that I could create a product that they would be happy with. That goes double for running a finishing funds campaign: To go back a second time, I really wanted to show how far we had come, and I think our current "official" trailer is leaps and bounds above the original teaser both in terms of content and visuals.

## Q. What should teams consider when putting together offers and rewards?

**A:** Would you want to purchase what you're offering? I know that rewards are listed as "perks," but honestly, I look at them more as items in a store. If $15 gets you a digital copy of the film, I think that is very affordable. That's why our most recent campaign essentially tops out at $150 contributions: I want people to look at what they can get and be excited about it. I don't want people to say "I wish I could afford to get the better version." I don't want to make this project for rich people only. I want to make an awesome movie that people can be proud to have helped create, so I want it to be accessible to everyone.

I also wanted to supply rewards that people actually want. T-shirts are great, but beyond that I wanted some big-ticket items as well. So we got arcade joysticks that were signed by pro gamers who appear in the film as well as a signed Xbox 360. They say you have to spend money to make money, so don't get stingy with things like posters and shirts… we found some great printers and created something that we would want to wear or hang in our house.

## Q. What one activity or reward seemed to generate the most response from the community? The least? Why?

**A:** Signed, limited edition items, or things with special features or extras seemed most successful. I was actually very surprised how many people gave us $300 to have their names hidden within the film – I'm sure that wasn't the only reason to contribute that amount, but I think it made people interested. We haven't had any negative feedback in terms of perks, but I will say that I was surprised at how many people decided to go with a physical copy of the film vs. the cheaper digital version. I really think it's all about them wanting to support the project and help us reach our goal. For our campaigns specifically, we've caught a lot more of the hardcore market than casual viewers, which I think is a large factor for why the $15 amount isn't that popular. (Note: After reaching our goal and hitting more mainstream sites like Wired.com and Yahoo.jp, the $15 option got more contributors.)

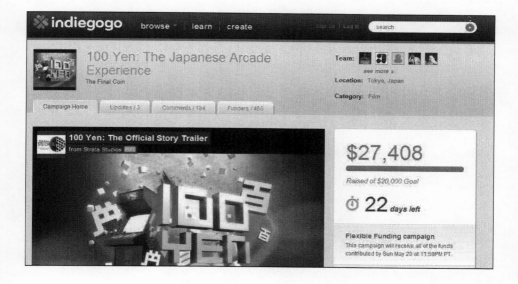

## Q. What PR and social media strategies did you use to get the word out about your campaign? Did you run them yourself, or did you hire a professional?

**A:** A little from Column A, and a little from Column B. The first run through it was all me plugging away via Facebook and through friends of friends. I would write poorly-worded (in retrospect) emails to websites and blogs in my spare time and just try to get news about the project out.

The second campaign was totally different: We hired a pro and had interviews lined up before day one even hit. We had websites redone and social media goals and targets. We now have physical press kits going out and are trying to line up screening dates so that as soon as the film is complete we can ramp up into full gear and get the news out to the world.

It's a full-time job to do it right – don't think that just by putting up a campaign online that it will generate interest and you'll get funded. You have to hustle and do it well to promote your campaign to the right news and media sites at the right time: Some will want exclusives and some won't take you seriously and some will keep delaying. Be aggressive in a polite and pro-fessional manner or hire a pro. It's a lot more work than it appears at first glance. Oh... and have a game plan before getting started: Weekly, daily, hourly... the more detailed the better. The more info you can provide and the more you interact with your fans, the better.

The best tool we used when conducting the campaign was Twinitor, a Twitter search en-gine. It was absolutely essential in my mind: I would have missed 75% of all our users' activity without it. Also take advantage of tools like Google Analytics and Vimeo Statistics... stats are key, so you know who's coming to your site, where they're coming from, and when. Find the source and celebrate it, spread news about it, and get people excited. Don't rely on Kickstarter or In-dieGoGo for marketing either: These services are amazing platforms and they absolutely have been a great help for my film, but they will not spread word about your project alone. Assume they are out to lunch and go out and tell people yourself.

# Q. What was it like after the campaign launched?

**A:** I got tons of emails asking questions and general inquiries about perks and so forth. Answering them is not unmanageable by any means, but make sure to reply to fans promptly, as they are the reason you're able to succeed at meeting your project goals and creat-ing end results. I try to update Facebook several times a week and point people to our page as the source for the newest info. Updates don't even have to be fully related to the project – just keep people in the loop. Email or Facebook are my preferred choices for communication. If I need addresses or other fan specifics, I'll send emails, but if an announcement is general and less important I'll post it on Facebook. IndieGoGo also has a great update system that you can post to in order to help get important news out.

Timing is everything here too. The first time around, we appeared on some major sites after the campaign had ended and missed some really big opportunities.  If I did it all over again, I would have had all of my promotional content prepared well in advance with a day-to-day schedule of updates and plans. I'd also hire a pro that knows your market or knows it better than you as well – it helps a lot.

# Q. Your final advice for future campaign creators would be...?

**A:** Having a rock-solid website in place is critical to help point people in the right direction rather than just the campaign page, which eventually becomes somewhat of a dead link. Also, know your audience, who they are, and where you can find them. Without this knowl-edge, I don't know if you'll be able to accomplish your goals. Do your research, make a list of media sites that might be interested, and find out who to contact there – don't just use random emails, but rather try to narrow down your targets.

# Scott Thomas – Creator of Designing Obama

The design director for the 2008 Obama presidential campaign, Scott Thomas was an early pioneer on Kickstarter with his *Designing Obama* campaign. At a time when few crowdfunding programs had caught the public's eye, and raising six-figure amounts through online pledges seemed just a pipe dream, he managed to pull in an impressive $84,613 for a historical book chronicling the art and design that helped propel Barack Obama into office. Intriguingly, Scott was also one of the first to encounter issues that new crowdfunding campaigns still encounter today. Here, he offers greater insight into the project, and advice to others hoping to follow his lead.

## Q. What does a design director for a political campaign do?

A: The responsibility of the team and myself was to design the presence of the Obama 2008 campaign both online and offline. So we handled much of the user interface design for the BarackObama.com and my.BarackObama.com websites, as well as a lot of the branding materials such as posters and banners that were used at events. We managed a lot of the visuals that you saw coming out of the campaign.

## Q. How did you come to assemble a book out of all of those materials? And why turn to crowdfunding?

A: Well, obviously it was a fairly defining moment in American history, and I'm a firm believer that if you do something large that you should a little time to come to terms with it. I wanted to chronicle some of the work that we did inside the campaign as well as the coinciding art and design movement that was happening outside the campaign. I felt that it was a pretty remarkable point in history where artists and graphic designers rallied around a presidential candidate. Typically the design and art industry is fairly pessimistic of world leaders and it's usually hard to rally them to a political cause.

As I began talking to publishers, I quickly realized that publishers suck. They were in it to produce their book and put my name on it. They weren't all that interested in me controlling the process, including one publisher that (when I stated that I wanted to do the design of the book myself) asked if they could review my design portfolio! At the end of the day, I really didn't see what benefit I would get from using a traditional publisher. I wanted to make an artifact; an object with my own spirit, and my own agenda. So I was toying with a lot of ideas as far as how to bring the book out, and luckily an individual from Kickstarter was in Chicago at that time. We ended up meeting up, and he told me what he was doing with Kickstarter and I thought it would be a perfect platform for the project.

**Q.** That was pretty early in Kickstarter's life, so there weren't all that many campaigns to study, and none that were for high-end design books such as this. How did you go about researching how you would put a campaign together?

**A:** My project was a bit unprecedented for Kickstarter at the time. I wanted to raise $100,000 for the project, and one of the folks at Kickstarter actually talked me down, saying, "I don't know that we can generate that much yet: I want you to succeed, I don't want this project to fail." And then he explained that you could go over your goal, and that was probably what would happen if I set the goal lower. So that's how we wound up at $65,000. But that was a hard decision for me to make, because I knew exactly how much the project was going to cost. (At least, I thought I did.) And I didn't have a lot to work off of, other than the fact that a video was going to be a good way of talking about what the thesis of the book was going to be, and planned to try to connect myself to it and to the project as a whole.

There was also a point in time where I wasn't sure I was going to have enough control over the platform. I wasn't sure that people were going to come to this site and "believe" in this Kickstarter idea, so I set up a separate website, DesigningObama.com, just to be able to tell the story a bit more and to make it seem a little more official, because it was so new to people at the time.

**Q.** What sort of PR and marketing did you do around the campaign?

**A:** I was doing a lecture tour at the time, speaking about my experience on the campaign, and I coupled that with the launch of the books. I launched it in New York City at the School for Visual Arts, which turned out to be a great platform to launch the project. And then I reached out to a lot of my friends and folks in my network and let them know I was launching this project, and mentioned to them that it would be great if they told folks on Twitter, and helped me spread the word. And I think that several of the folks in the design community that I reached out to ended up starting their own project campaigns later on, such as Scott Wilson at MINIMAL and the TikTok watch kit.

A lot of what I did was reach out to my friends who I knew had large followings on social networks, and had them post or tweet about the project as well. For me, Twitter was pretty much the most fundamental part of the marketing that I did. I think it is what really powered the level of support we garnered for the campaign.

The rewards I created were primarily going to revolve around the book, and that was what I wanted to keep the focus on, rather than creating all sort of other incentives for backing the project. And at the time there really wasn't all that much precedent for having a more complex ladder of rewards. The other thing that I knew and understood was that the more complexity in the rewards, the more cost and difficulty there would be in fulfilling them at the end. I knew the book was going to be a huge challenge just by itself. Even the three different books that I had proved to be too complicated: In hindsight, I wish I'd only done one version and left it at that.

## Q. How much time did you spend interacting with the community once the campaign was running?

A: A lot, actually. It was so early in the life of Kickstarter that people didn't really understand how the whole thing worked. They assumed that the book had already been produced, already been printed, and were asking why it hadn't shipped yet. Lots of folks didn't realize that it wasn't actually done yet. I had a few renders of the book, and a table of contents, and some of the writing was done, but I was nowhere even close to having the book finished. There were many people who were backing the project, even when it was about to close, wondering, "Where's my book?" So I spent a lot of time responding to messages about that, explaining what Kickstarter was, and how the platform worked. And then there was the problem of shipping and fulfillment.

*Designing Obama* was, for its time, unusual in that it had an unprecedented number of international project backers. And the book weighs five pounds. So when you walk into the post office in downtown Chicago and say, "I'd like to ship five hundred of these overseas. How do I go about doing that?" Well, let's just say the folks there were not the most informative bunch when confronted with the challenge of shipping paper by the ton. So I had to go back to all of the backers and explain that the cost did not include shipping, and we'd have to settle that up separately when the books were done and ready to ship. This was a part of the process, that, in hindsight, I simply didn't know enough about.

Fulfillment companies are fairly used to this, but I did it pretty raw, to the point where I was renting trucks, I was loading pallets, and I was packing books with friends and family. And I did it all to keep the shipping costs down and not upset my backers. I do not recommend this as a strategy, but this is what I ended up having to do.

## Q. What advice would you have for teams that are putting together a campaign now about how to get the word out?

**A:** I would strongly suggest that you reach out to your community. If you can convince them that this is a cool project and something of interest, then word about it just naturally spreads. And I think that is the fundamental way to involve people and to get them to back you and support your project.

## Q. After the campaign was over, how did you maintain contact with backers?

**A:** I predominantly used updates on the Kickstarter page to just let people know where we were at in the process, how fulfillment was going, and post the occasional "woe is me" update about the difficulties of writing a book. Sometimes it was challenging because commenters online have a tendency to comment in ways that may sound negative, and that can sometimes be a blow to your self-esteem, or your confidence in the project. Comments would include the likes of "Why is this taking so long?" And I'd have to post an update and explain that I was designing, writing, publishing and fulfilling a book myself. Just me. So there were some times that I just had to get away, go home, sleep, and then come back refreshed before I wrote a response.

## Q. Any last thoughts you'd like to leave today's crowdfunders with?

**A:** With a lot of these projects, you don't think to build in a salary for yourself. You think "I'm just going to do this project and it's going to be cool," and then you realize that you still have to work a day job on top of it. So I had to take on freelance work, but that ended up taking time away from getting the book done. When plotting a campaign, think through the process, from end to end, and all of the associated costs that go along with it. That way, when you have to move two tons of paper from your garage to points all over the world, you have a plan for how to do it. Also, if you can do the project as a part of a team, it's far better than trying to do it yourself. This was one of my really important pieces of learning. I really wanted to do the project myself, but looking back I would have been far better off if I had involved more people in it.

# ABOUT SCOTT STEINBERG

AUTHOR | SPEAKER | CONSULTANT | SPOKESPERSON | EXPERT WITNESS

Technology expert and serial entrepreneur Scott Steinberg is the CEO of business consulting and product testing firm TechSavvy Global, and one of today's most trusted advisors to both small businesses and the world's largest brands. The creator of the bestselling The Modern Parent's Guide and The Business Expert's Guidebook series, and among the industry's most celebrated strategic consultants, keynote speakers and expert witnesses, he's been hailed as a leading expert on enterprise management and startup culture by dozens of publications from NPR to The Wall St. Journal. A regular on-air authority for all major TV networks including ABC, CBS, FOX, NBC and CNN, he's covered the field for 400+ outlets from The New York Times to Wired, and served as an industry insider for Fast Company, Entrepreneur, The Los Angeles Times, Rolling Stone and more.

As a top motivational and business speaker, he's presented and hosted events for governments, Fortune 500 corporations and industry trade groups worldwide. Steinberg further aids industry leaders, attorneys and investors with business strategy consulting, expert witness testimony and market analysis. Among the world's most-quoted business, technology, social media and consumer products analysts, he's also a nationally-syndicated business columnist for Inc. magazine, and makes regular appearances as Sears Toy Shop's toy tech expert. Besides serving as an executive coach, motivational guest speaker and management consultant, he additionally hosts several popular video shows including Tech Industry Insider, Business Expert, Family Tech, Gear Up and Game Theory. The author of over half a dozen books on business, marketing and technology, his companies publish software, websites, magazines, films and more. Between public speaking ops, instructional videos, articles and podcasts, he remains one of the industry's most outspoken DIY evangelists and advocates for continuing education.

For more info, see www.ASmallBusinessExpert.com or follow him on Twitter (@GadgetExpert).

# About Rusel DeMaria

Rusel DeMaria has been following the game industry for 40 years as a gamer, writer, analyst, designer and consultant. He has been a senior editor and columnist for several national and international magazines and was the founding editor and creative director for the successful strategy guide series from Prima Publishing. Among his best-known books are *High Score: The Illustrated History of Electronic Games*, *Reset: Changing the Way We Look at Video Games*, and *David Perry on Game Design* (for which he was principal author and researcher).

# About Jon Kimmich

Games industry expert Jon Kimmich has been an author, instructor, strategic advisor and consultant to companies, individuals and investors in the games industry for over 15 years. He started his career in digital entertainment as a Planner for Microsoft during pivotal parts of the Xbox conception and launch, and was instrumental in the acquisition of many firms for Microsoft Games Studios including Bungie and FASA Interactive; hit games such as *Dungeon Siege*, *Rise of Nations* and *MechAssault;* and internally-developed games like *Crimson Skies* and *Halo*. Now Jon works with development studios, publishers, educators and investors to incubate and drive strategic innovation in content and business models in the mobile and digital entertainment sectors.

20197476R00051

Made in the USA
Lexington, KY
24 January 2013